Best
Garden Plants
for
Illinois

William Aldrich • Don Williamson

LONE PINE

Lone Pine Publishing International

The Distributer: Lone Pine Publishing
1808 B Street NW, Suite 140
Auburn, WA, USA 98001
Website: www.lonepinepublishing.com

Library and Archives Canada Cataloguing in Publication

Aldrich, William, 1948–
    Best garden plants for Illinois / William Aldrich, Don Williamson.

ISBN–13: 978–1–55105–502–2
ISBN–10: 1–55105–502–3

    1. Plants, Ornamental—Illinois. 2. Gardening—Illinois.
I. Williamson, Don, 1962– II. Title.

SB453.2.I3A426 2006   635'.09773   C2005–907062–5

Scanning & Digital Film: Elite Lithographers Co.

Front cover photographs by Tamara Eder and Tim Matheson except where noted. *Clockwise from top right:* climbing rose 'New Dawn,' crabapple blossom, iris, lilac leaves, daylily, sweet potato vine, hybrid tea 'Just Joey,' lily (Laura Peters), columbine, lily (Erika Flatt)

Photography: All photography by Tim Matheson and Tamara Eder except:
Sandra Bit 92a; David Cavagnaro 166a&b; Chicagoland Grows Inc. 75a; Joan de Grey 42a; Don Doucette 97b, 104b; Jen Fafard 133a; Derek Fell 41b, 107a; Erika Flatt 9b, 90a, 129b, 134a, 164b; Anne Gordon 59b; Saxon Holt 116a; Duncan Kelbaugh 129a; Debra Knapke 124a; Marilynn McAra 133b; Dawn Loewen 71a, 76a, 168a; Kim Patrick O'Leary 19a&b, 128a, 131a, 141b; Steve Nikkila 59a; Allison Penko 10b, 41a, 50a, 71b, 72a, 74a, 89b, 91a, 92b, 96a&b, 99a, 100a&b, 103a&b, 118b, 120b, 121b, 123a, 128b, 132a, 147a, 149b, 150b, 157a, 159a&b, 160a&b, 162a, 163b; Laura Peters 9a, 10a, 17a, 40a&b, 54a&b, 67a&b, 69a&b, 73a, 75b, 77a, 85a, 87a&b, 94a, 114a, 115a, 118a, 134b, 136a&b, 137b, 138a&b 139a&b, 142a&b, 143a&b, 144a&b, 147b, 148a, 149a, 150a, 151a&b, 157b, 158a&b, 162b, 163a, 164a, 167a&b, 169a&b; Photos.com 135a; Robert Ritchie 39b, 43a, 70b, 81a&b, 84a, 93a&b, 95a, 113a, 122a, 141a; Leila Sidi 135b; Peter Thompstone 21a, 48a, 57a&b, 60a; Valleybrook Gardens 62a; Don Williamson 130a&b, 137a; Tim Wood 70a, 104a, 106a.

PC: P13

Table of Contents

Introduction

Starting a garden can seem like a daunting task. Which plants should you choose? Where should you put them in the garden? How many of us can say we have used the term "brown thumb" to describe our previous failures in the garden?

This book is intended to give beginning gardeners the information they need to have success in planning and planting gardens. It describes a wide variety of plants and provides basic information such as where and how to plant. It isn't guaranteed to give you a green thumb, but it will give you the understanding to be able to succeed.

Illinois exhibits a wide diversity of ecological regions and each presents its own unique challenges. One of the biggest challenges is selecting plants that can handle our climate, especially our cold winters. USDA hardiness zones are based on annual average minimum temperatures. Plants are rated based on the zones in which they grow successfully, but cold is not the only factor that influences winter survival. A winter temperature of –5° F

is very different with snow cover than without; in soggy soil or in dry; following a hot summer or a long, cold, wet one. These factors will have more influence on the survival of plants than will temperature.

Spring and fall frost dates are often used when discussing climate and gardening. They give us a general idea of when the last chance of frost is in spring and the first chance of frost is in fall. The last-frost date in spring combined with the first-frost date in fall allows us to predict the length of the growing season. Your local garden center should be able to provide you with local hardiness zones and frost date information.

Getting Started
When planning your garden, start with a quick analysis of the garden as it is now. Plants have specific requirements, and it is best to put the right plant in the right place rather than to change your garden to suit the plants you want.

Knowing which parts of your garden receive the most and least amounts of sunlight will help you choose the proper plants and decide where to plant them. Light is classified into four basic groups: full sun (direct, unobstructed light all or most of the day); partial shade (direct sun for about half the day and shade for the rest); light shade (shade all or most of the day with some sun filtering through to ground level); and full shade (no direct sunlight). Most plants prefer a certain amount of light, but many can adapt to a range of light levels.

Plants use the soil to hold themselves upright but also rely on the many resources it holds: air, water, nutrients, organic matter and a host of microbes. The particle size of the soil influences the amount of air, water and nutrients it can hold. Sand, with the largest particles, has a lot of air space and allows water and nutrients to drain quickly. Clay, with the smallest particles, is high in nutrients but has very little air space. Water is therefore slow to penetrate clay and slow to drain from it.

Soil acidity or alkalinity (measured on the pH scale) influences what nutrients are available to plants. A pH of 7 is neutral; a lower pH is more acidic. Most plants prefer a soil with a pH of 5.5–7.5. Soil-testing kits are available at most garden centers, and soil samples can be sent to testing facilities for a more thorough analysis.

Compost is one of the best and most important amendments you can add to any type of soil. Compost improves soil by adding organic matter and nutrients, introducing soil microbes, increasing water retention and improving drainage. Compost can be purchased or you can make it in your own backyard.

Microclimates are small areas that are generally warmer or colder than the surrounding area. Buildings, fences, trees and other large structures can provide extra shelter in winter but may trap heat in summer, thus creating a warmer microclimate. The bottoms of hills are

Hardiness Zones Map

Average Annual Minimum Temperature

Zone	Temp (°F)
4b	−20 to −25
5a	−15 to −20
5b	−10 to −15
6a	−5 to −10
6b	0 to −5

usually colder than the tops but may not be as windy. Take advantage of these areas when you plan your garden and choose your plants; you may even grow out-of-zone plants successfully in a warm, sheltered location.

Selecting Plants

It's important to purchase healthy plants that are free of pests and diseases. Such plants will establish quickly in your garden and won't introduce problems that may spread to other plants. You should have a good idea of what the plant is supposed to look like—the color and shape of the leaves and the habit of the plant—and then inspect the plant for signs of disease or infestation.

The most efficient way for nurseries and greenhouses to grow plants is in containers, but raising plants in a restricted space for too long can cause the roots to densely encircle the insides of the pots. These pot-bound plants are often stressed and can take longer to establish, if they establish at all. If possible, before buying a plant gently remove the pot to see the condition of the roots and to check for soil-borne insects.

Planting Basics

The following tips apply to all plants:

- Prepare the garden before planting. Dig over the soil, pull up any weeds and make any needed amendments before you begin planting if you are starting a new landscape. This may be more difficult in established beds to which you want to add a single plant. The prepared area should be at least twice the size of the plant you want to put in, and preferably the expected size of the mature plant.

- Settle the soil with water. Good contact between the roots and the soil is important, but if you press the soil down too firmly, as often happens when you step on it, you can cause compaction, which reduces the movement of water through the soil and leaves very few air spaces. Instead, pour water in as you fill the hole with soil. The water will settle the soil evenly without allowing it to compact.

- Unwrap the roots. It is always best to remove any container before planting to give roots the chance to spread out naturally when planted. In particular, you should remove plastic containers, fiber pots, wire and burlap before planting trees. Fiber pots decompose very slowly, if at all, and wick moisture away from the plant. Synthetic burlap won't decompose, and wire can strangle the roots as they mature. The only exceptions to this rule are peat pots and pellets used to start annuals and vegetables; these decompose and can be planted with the young transplants.

Gently remove container.

Ensure proper planting depth.

Backfill with soil.

- Accommodate the rootball. If you prepared your planting spot ahead of time, your planting hole will only need to be big enough to accommodate the rootball with the roots spread out slightly.

- Know the mature size. Place your plants based on how big the plants will grow rather than how big they are when you plant them. Large plants should have enough room to mature without interfering with walls, roof overhangs, power lines and walkways.

- Plant at the same depth in the soil. Plants generally like to grow at a specific level in relation to the soil and should be planted at the same level they were growing at before you transplanted them.

- Identify your plants. Keep track of what's what in your garden by putting a tag next to your plant when you plant it, or by making an overhead drawing with plant names and locations. It is very easy to forget exactly what you planted and where you planted it.

- Water deeply and infrequently. It's better to water deeply once every week or two rather than to water lightly more often. Deep watering forces roots to grow as they search for water and helps them survive dry spells when water bans may restrict your watering regime. Always check the rootzone before you water. More gardeners overwater than underwater.

Annuals

Annuals are only expected to last for a single growing season. Their flowers and decorative foliage provide bright splashes of color and can fill in spaces around immature trees, shrubs and perennials.

Annuals are easy to plant and are usually sold in small packs of four or six. The roots quickly fill the space in these small packs, so the small rootball should be broken up before planting. For most annuals, you can split the ball in two up the center or run your thumb up each side to break up the roots.

Many annuals are grown from seed and can be started directly in the garden. Plants that dislike having their roots disturbed are often grown directly from seed or grown in peat pots or pellets to minimize root disturbance. Consult an annual book such as Lone Pine's *Annuals for Illinois* for further information on the care and growing of annuals.

Perennials

Perennials grow for three or more years. They usually die back to the ground each fall and send up new shoots in spring, though some are evergreen. They often have a shorter period of bloom than annuals but require less care.

Many perennials benefit from being divided every few years. This keeps them growing and blooming vigorously, and in

Settle backfilled soil with water.

Water the plant well.

Add a layer of mulch.

some cases controls their spread. Dividing involves digging the plant up, removing dead bits, breaking the plant into several pieces and replanting some or all of the pieces. Extra pieces can be given as gifts to family, friends and neighbors. Consult a perennial book such as Lone Pine's *Perennials for Illinois* for further information on the care of perennials.

Trees & Shrubs

Trees and shrubs provide the bones of the garden. They are often the slowest growing plants but usually live the longest. Characterized by leaf type, they may be deciduous or evergreen, and needled or broad-leaved.

Trees should have as little disturbed soil as possible at the bottom of the planting hole. Loose dirt settles over time, and sinking even an inch can kill some trees.

Staking, sometimes recommended for newly planted trees, is only necessary for trees over 5' tall.

Pruning is more often required for shrubs than trees. It helps them maintain an attractive shape and can improve blooming. It is a good idea to take a pruning course or to hire or consult with an ISA (International Society of Arboriculture)

Trees and shrubs provide backbone to the mixed border.

Training vines to climb arbors adds structure to the garden.

certified arborist if you have never pruned before. Consult Lone Pine's *Tree and Shrub Gardening for Illinois* for information about pruning trees and shrubs.

Roses

Roses are beautiful shrubs with lovely, often-fragrant blooms. Traditionally, most roses only bloomed once in the growing season, but new varieties bloom all, or almost all, summer.

Generally, roses prefer a fertile, well-prepared planting area. A rule of thumb is to prepare a circular area 24" in diameter and deep. Add plenty of compost or other fertile organic matter and keep roses well watered during the growing season. Many roses are quite durable and will adapt to poorer conditions. Roses, like all shrubs, have specific pruning requirements.

Vines

Vines or climbing plants are useful for screening and shade, especially in a location too small for a tree. They may be woody or herbaceous and annual or perennial.

Most vines need sturdy supports to grow up on. Trellises, arbors, porch railings, fences, walls, poles and trees are all possible supports. If a support is needed, ensure it's in place before you plant to avoid disturbing the roots later.

Vines and plants that are aggressive spreaders make excellent groundcovers, but any plant with dense growth will serve the purpose if planted in large numbers. Space plants closer together when planting to ensure the ground is completely covered.

Bulbs

These plants have fleshy underground storage organs that allow them to survive extended periods of dormancy. They are often grown for the bright splashes of color their flowers provide. They may be spring, summer or fall flowering.

Hardy bulbs can be left in the ground and will flower every year, but many popular tender plants grow from bulbs, corms or tubers. These tender plants are generally lifted from the garden in fall as the foliage dies back and are stored in a cool, frost-free location for winter, to be replanted in spring.

Lilies bloom throughout the summer.

Many herbs grow well in pots.

Herbs

Herbs may be medicinal or culinary and are often both. A few common culinary herbs are listed in this book. Even if you don't cook with them, the often-fragrant foliage adds its aroma to the garden, and the plants have decorative forms, leaves and flowers.

Many herbs have pollen-producing flowers that attract butterflies, bees and hummingbirds. They also attract predatory insects. These useful insects help to manage your pest problems by feasting on problem insects such as aphids, mealy bugs and whiteflies.

Ferns, Grasses & Foliage Plants

Foliage is an important consideration when choosing plants for your garden. Although many plants look spectacular in bloom, they can seem rather dull without flowers. Including a variety of plants with unique, interesting, or striking foliage can provide all the color and texture you want without the need to rely on flowers.

Ferns are ancient plants that have adapted to many different environments. The fern family is a very large group of plants with interesting foliage in a wide array of shapes and colors. Ferns do not produce flowers, but instead reproduce by spores borne in interesting structures on the undersides and margins of the foliage. Ferns are generally planted in moist, shaded gardens, but some will thrive in dry shade under the deep shade of some trees, such as beech and magnolia.

Ornamental grasses are becoming very popular garden additions. Grasses offer a variety of textures and foliage colors, and at least three seasons of interest. There is an ornamental grass for every garden situation and condition. Some grasses will thrive in any garden condition, from hot and dry to cool and wet, and in all types of soils.

Ornamental grasses have very few insect or disease problems. They require very little maintenance other than cutting the perennial grasses back in fall or spring.

Ornamental grasses add color, variety and texture.

If you plan to leave dried grass standing for winter interest, be aware that it can present a fire hazard. Dry grass is highly flammable and should be cut back in fall if it is near a house or other structure.

Basically any plant that covers the ground can be used as a groundcover. Groundcovers are often spreading plants with dense growth that are used to control soil erosion, to keep weeds at bay and to fill garden areas that are difficult to maintain. Groundcovers can be herbaceous or woody and annual or perennial.

We have included a variety of plants grown for their foliage throughout this book. Many annuals, perennials, trees, shrubs, vines and herbs have wonderful foliage, and will be an asset to your garden landscape.

Final Comments

We encourage you to visit the outstanding garden shows, county fairs, public gardens, arboretums and private gardens (get permission first) we have here in Illinois to see what plants grows best and if any plants catch your interest. A walk through your neighborhood is also a great way to see what plants might do well in your own garden. Don't be afraid to ask questions.

Every county in the state has an office of the University of Illinois Extension. Their resources are vast and respected. Check out their online site at http://www.extension.uiuc.edu or look in the White Pages of the phone book under University of Illinois for your county's office.

Also don't be afraid to experiment. No matter how many books you read, trying things yourself is the best way to learn and to find out what will grow in your garden. Use the information provided as a guideline, and have fun!

Angelonia
Angelonia

A. angustifolia cultivars (above & below)

Take your pick on what the small blooms remind you of—pseudo snapdragon, orchid or an angel. Angelonias are lush, heat-loving plants with multiple blooms on upright stems in many shades of blue, pink and white.

Growing

Angelonia prefers **full sun** but tolerates a bit of shade. The soil should be **fertile, moist** and **well drained**. Although this plant grows naturally in damp areas, such as along ditches and near ponds, it is fairly drought and heat tolerant. Plant out after the chance of frost has passed.

Tips

Angelonia makes a good addition to an annual or mixed border where it is most attractive when planted in groups. It is also suited to a pondside or streamside planting.

Recommended

A. angustifolia is a bushy, upright plant with loose spikes of flowers in varied shades of purple. Cultivars with white or bicolored flowers are available. **Angelface Series** (from Proven Winners) bear larger flowers and are more compact than the species, reaching 12–18" in height. **Angelmist Series** (from Simply Beautiful) are strong growers, reaching 18–24" in height, and are fine cut flowers.

The individual flowers look a bit like orchid blossoms, but angelonia is actually in the same family as snapdragon.

Also called: angel wings, summer snapdragon **Features:** attractive, purple, blue, white, bicolored flowers
Height: 12–24" **Spread:** 12"

Bacopa
Sutera

S. cordata (above & below)

Bacopa is a perennial that is grown as an annual outdoors. It will thrive as a houseplant in a bright room.

Few plants can dazzle as well as bacopa. Cascading over the sides of a hanging basket, a well-grown bacopa sports a dense carpet of tiny, white to pale lavender flowers. But there is a downside; bacopa likes to be kept moist and will need fertilizer every two or three weeks to keep up that blast of blooming.

Growing

Bacopa grows well in **partial shade** with protection from the hot afternoon sun. The soil should be of **average fertility, humus rich, moist** and **well drained**.

Don't allow this plant to dry out, or the leaves will quickly die. Cutting back dead growth may encourage new shoots to form.

Tips

Bacopa is a popular plant for hanging baskets, mixed containers and window boxes. It is not recommended as a bedding plant because it fizzles quickly when the weather gets hot, particularly if you forget to water. Plant it where you will see it every day so you will remember to water it.

Recommended

S. cordata is a compact, trailing plant that bears small, white flowers all summer. Cultivars with larger, white or lavender flowers or gold and green variegated foliage are available.

Features: decorative, white or lavender flowers; foliage; habit **Height:** 3–6" **Spread:** 12–20"

Begonia
Begonia

Veteran gardeners may overlook the venerable wax begonias in favor of the more spectacular rexes or the more challenging tuberous begonias, but all deserve their spots in the garden.

Growing

Begonias grow best in **light or partial shade** in **fertile, well-drained, neutral to acidic** soil that is **rich in organic matter**. Some wax begonias tolerate sun if the soil is kept moist. Allow the soil to dry out slightly between waterings, particularly for tuberous begonias. Don't plant begonias before the soil warms in spring. In cold soil they may fail to thrive. For tuberous begonias, plant tubers concave side up.

Tips

All begonias are useful for shaded garden beds and planters. Trailing tuberous varieties look great when their flowers are allowed to cascade down. Wax begonias are attractive as edging plants. Rex begonias, with their dramatic foliage, and Dragon Wing are useful as specimen plants.

Recommended

B. x *hybrida* **Dragon Wing** bears deep scarlet to deep pink flowers and angel-winged foliage. It is heat tolerant.

B. Rex Cultorum **Hybrids** (rex begonias) are grown for their dramatic, colorful foliage.

B. Rex Cultorum hybrids 'Escargot' (above)
B. x tuberhybrida (below)

B. semperflorens (wax begonias) has pink, white, red or bicolored flowers and green, bronze, reddish or white-variegated foliage.

B. x *tuberhybrida* (tuberous begonias) are generally sold as tubers. The flowers come in many shades of red, pink, yellow, orange or white.

Features: pink, white, red, yellow, orange, bicolored, picotee flowers; decorative foliage; easy to grow; low maintenance
Height: 6–24" **Spread:** 6–24"

Celosia

Celosia

C. *argentea* Plumosa Group (above)
C. *argentea* Cristata Group (below)

If you've never grown a true cockscomb, give it a shot—you'll love the novelty of the amazing flower head. On the other end of the spectrum are the wheat celosias, with airy, feather-like flower spikes.

Growing

A sheltered spot in **full sun** is best for celosia. The soil should be **fertile, moist** and **well drained**, with plenty of **organic matter** worked in.

Celosia grows best when directly sown in the garden. If starting indoors, seed in peat pots or pellets and plant them, and nursery-purchased plants, before they begin to flower. Keep seeds moist while they are germinating, and do not cover them.

Tips

Celosia works well in borders, beds and planters. The flowers make interesting additions to fresh or dried arrangements. Crested varieties work well as accents and as cut flowers.

Recommended

C. argentea **Cristata Group** (crested celosia, cockscomb) has blooms that resemble brains or rooster combs. **Plumosa Group** (plume celosia) has plume-like blooms. Both groups have many varieties and cultivars.

C. spicata (*C. argentea* Spicata Group; wheat celosia) flowers often have a metallic sheen. **'Flamingo Feather'** has slender spikes of pink to white flowers. **'Flamingo Purple'** bears spikes of purple to white flowers and dark red-green stems and leaves.

Features: intensely colorful, interesting, red, orange, gold, yellow, pink, purple flowers
Height: 6"–4' **Spread:** equal to or slightly less than height

Cleome
Cleome

C. hassleriana Royal Queen Series (above), *C. hassleriana* (below)

Create a bold and exotic display in your garden with these lovely and unusual flowers.

Growing

Cleomes prefer **full sun** but tolerate partial shade. Any kind of soil will do fine. Mix in plenty of **organic matter** to help the soil retain moisture. Cleomes are drought tolerant but perform better if watered regularly. Overwatering causes leggy plants.

Pinch out the tip of the center stem on young plants to encourage branching and more blooms. Deadhead to prolong blooming and to reduce prolific self-seeding.

Tips

Cleome can be planted in groups at the back of a border or in the center of an island bed. It also makes an attractive addition to mixed containers.

Recommended

C. hassleriana is a tall, upright plant with strong, supple, thorny stems. The foliage and flowers have a strong scent. '**Helen Campbell**' has white flowers. **Royal Queen Series** are fade-resistant plants that bloom in white, pink or violet purple. '**Sparkler Blush**' is a dwarf cultivar with pink flowers that fade to white. '**Sparkler Rose**' is also dwarf, bearing deep pink flowers that resist fading.

C. '**Linde Armstrong**' is a compact, thornless, heat-tolerant variety with rosy pink blooms.

C. serrulata (Rocky Mountain Bee Plant) '**Solo**' is thornless, grows 12–18" tall and bears large pink and white blooms.

Features: attractive, scented foliage; purple, pink, white flowers; thorny stems
Height: 10"–5' **Spread:** 12–36"

Cosmos

Cosmos

C. bipinnatus (above & below)

Cosmos have reached an exalted status in American gardening—no self-respecting annual garden should be without them.

Growing

Cosmos like **full sun** and **well-drained** soil with **poor to average fertility**. Plant out after the last frost. Overfertilizing and overwatering can reduce the number of flowers. Cut faded blooms to encourage more buds. These plants often self-seed.

Tips

Cosmos are care-free, colorful, lacy, drought-tolerant plants that make an attractive addition to cottage gardens and the backs of borders, and can be mass planted in informal beds and borders.

To avoid staking, plant cosmos against a fence or in a sheltered location, or grow shorter varieties. Push twiggy branches into the ground when the plants are young and allow them to grow up between the branches. The mature plant will hide the branches.

Recommended

C. atrosanguineus (chocolate cosmos) is an upright plant with fragrant, dark maroon flowers that some claim smell like chocolate.

C. bipinnatus (annual cosmos) is an erect plant with fine, fern-like foliage. It and its many cultivars bear magenta, rose, pink, white or bicolored flowers, usually with yellow centers.

C. sulphureus (yellow cosmos) is a smaller, denser plant than *C. bipinnatus*, and has gold, orange, scarlet or yellow flowers. Sow directly in the garden. Many cultivars are available.

Features: magenta, rose, pink, purple, white, yellow, orange, scarlet flowers; fern-like foliage; easy to grow; low maintenance
Height: 1–7' **Spread:** 12–18"

Geranium
Pelargonium

The stock trade of the bedding plant industry, geraniums suffer only from garden snobs who find them too common. The ivy-leaved types are great in hanging baskets. And then there are the scented geraniums— a world unto themselves.

Growing

Geraniums prefer **full sun** but tolerate partial shade, though they may not bloom as profusely. The soil should be **fertile** and **well drained**.

Deadheading is essential to keep geraniums blooming and looking neat.

P. x *hortorum* Fireworks Collection (above)
P. *peltatum* (below)

Tips

Geraniums are very popular for borders, beds, planters, hanging baskets and window boxes.

Geraniums are perennials that are treated as annuals and can be kept indoors over the winter in a bright room.

Recommended

P. x *hortorum* (zonal geranium) is a bushy plant with red, pink, purple, orange or white flowers and, frequently, banded or multi-colored foliage. Many cultivars are available.

P. peltatum (ivy-leaved geranium) has thick, waxy leaves and a trailing habit. Many cultivars are available.

P. species and **cultivars** (scented geraniums, scented pelargoniums) is a large group of geraniums that have scented leaves. The scents are grouped into the categories of rose, mint, citrus, fruit, spice or pungent.

Visit a plant trial facility to see how many Pelargonium *varieties are being tested and compared. You'll discover that it is always possible to improve on a good plant.*

Features: red, pink, violet, orange, salmon, white, purple flowers; decorative or scented foliage; variable habits **Height:** 8–24" **Spread:** 6"–4'

Impatiens

Impatiens

I. walleriana (above), *I. hawkeri* (below)

One of the most-asked questions in gardening is how to get more color in shady areas without planting the old standby impatiens. The answer: try one of the impatiens types you haven't considered before.

Growing

Impatiens do best in **partial or light shade** but tolerate full shade, and some tolerate full sun if kept moist. The soil should be **fertile, humus rich, moist** and **well drained**.

Tips

Mass plant impatiens in beds under trees, along shady fences and walls or in porch planters. They also look lovely in hanging baskets.

Recommended

I. balsamina (balsam impatiens) blooms in shades of purple, red, pink or white. It is the best impatiens for sun. There are several double-flowered cultivars.

I. hawkeri (New Guinea Hybrids; New Guinea impatiens) flowers in shades of red, orange, pink, purple or white. The foliage is often variegated with a yellow stripe down the center of each leaf. It can take more sun than *I. walleriana*.

I. Seashell Series are compact plants with flowers in shades of yellow, orange, apricot or pink.

I. walleriana (impatiens, busy Lizzie) flowers in shades of purple, red, burgundy, pink, yellow, salmon, orange, apricot, white or can be bicolored. Hundreds of cultivars are available.

Features: colorful flowers in shades of purple, red, burgundy, pink, yellow, salmon, orange, apricot, white, bicolored; grows well in shade
Height: 6–36" **Spread:** 8–24"

Lantana
Lantana

Lantanas gain popularity every year because of their range and combination of colors along with their low-maintenance requirements. Their informal, sprawling habit adds to their charm, as does their ability to attract butterflies.

Growing

Lantana grows best in **full sun** but tolerates partial shade. The soil should be **fertile, moist** and **well drained**. Plants are heat and drought tolerant. Cuttings can be taken in late summer and grown indoors for the winter so you will have plants the following summer.

Tips

Lantana is a tender shrub that is grown as an annual. It makes an attractive addition to beds and borders as well as in mixed containers and hanging baskets.

Recommended

L. camara is a bushy plant that bears round clusters of flowers in a variety of colors. The flowers often change color as they mature, giving the flower clusters a striking, multi-colored appearance. **'Spreading Sunset'** bears brightly colored orange to red flowers.

L. Patriot Series have plants that flower in a wide range of colors and have minty, dark to mid-green foliage.

L. camara 'Spreading Sunset' (above & below)

Lantanas are not intimidated by hot, dry weather, and a 3" bedding plant can reach the size of a small shrub in a single season.

Also called: shrub verbena
Features: stunning, yellow, orange, pink, purple, red, white flowers, often in combination; easy to grow; low maintenance **Height:** 2"–3½'
Spread: 1–3 ½'

Marigold
Tagetes

T. patula 'Boy Series' (above), *T. patula* hybrid (below)

Deadhead to prolong blooming and to keep plants tidy. *T. erecta* definitely needs to be deadheaded so that the fading flowers don't decay and set off a gray mold infection.

Tips
Mass planted or mixed with other plants, marigolds make a vibrant addition to beds, borders and container gardens. These plants thrive in the hottest, driest parts of your garden.

Recommended
There are many cultivars available for all the species. *T. erecta* (African marigold, American marigold, Aztec marigold) is the largest plant with the biggest flowers; *T. patula* (French marigold) is low growing and has a wide range of flower colors; *T. tenuifolia* (signet marigold) has become more popular recently because of its feathery foliage and small, dainty flowers; ***T. Triploid Hybrids*** (triploid marigold) have been developed by crossing French and African marigolds, which results in plants with huge flowers and compact growth.

For every self-proclaimed brown-thumb gardener, there is a marigold ready, willing and waiting to grow.

Growing
Marigolds grow best in **full sun**. The soil should be of **average fertility** and **well drained**. These plants are drought tolerant and hold up well in windy, rainy weather.

Features: bright yellow, red, orange, brown, gold, cream, bicolored flowers; fragrant foliage; easy to grow **Height:** 6–36" **Spread:** 12–24"

Million Bells

Calibrachoa

*C*alibrachoa hybrids have hit the market running because they are so floriferous. These low-growing, compact, vigorous plants tolerate our summer heat and require no deadheading. Feed them often, especially when grown in hanging baskets and planters.

Growing

Million bells prefers **full sun**. The soil should be **fertile, moist** and **well drained**. Although it prefers to be watered regularly, million bells is fairly drought resistant once established.

C. 'Trailing Blue' (above)
C. 'Trailing Pink' and 'Trailing Blue' (below)

Tips

Popular for planters and hanging baskets, million bells is also attractive in beds and borders. It grows all summer and needs plenty of room to spread, or it will overtake other flowers. Pinch the plants back to keep them compact.

Million bells blooms well into fall; the flowers become hardier as the weather cools, and plants can survive temperatures down to 20° F.

Recommended

Calibrachoa **Hybrids** have a dense, trailing habit. They bear small flowers that look like petunias. The **Superbells Series** is noted for its superior disease resistance and wide range of uniquely colored flowers.

Also called: trailing petunia
Features: pink, purple, yellow, red-orange, white, blue flowers; trailing habit
Height: 6–12" **Spread:** up to 24"

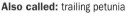

Nasturtium

Tropaeolum

T. majus (above), T. majus 'Alaska' (below)

Growing

Nasturtiums prefer **full sun** but tolerate some shade. The soil should be of **poor to average fertility, light, moist** and **well drained**. Soil that is too rich or has too much nitrogen fertilizer will result in lots of leaves and very few flowers. Let the soil drain completely between waterings. In the heat of summer, it is important to keep the plants well watered. Sow directly in the garden once the danger of frost has passed.

Tips

Nasturtiums are used in beds, borders, containers and hanging baskets and on sloped banks. The climbing varieties are grown up trellises, over rock walls or in places that need concealing. These plants thrive in poor locations, and they make an interesting addition to plantings on hard-to-mow slopes.

Recommended

T. majus has a trailing habit, but many of the cultivars have bushier, more refined habits. Cultivars offer differing flower colors or variegated foliage.

These fast-growing plants with brightly colored flowers are easy to grow, making them popular with beginners and experienced gardeners alike.

The leaves and flowers are edible, adding a peppery flavor to salads.

Features: red, orange, yellow, burgundy, pink, cream, gold, white, bicolored flowers; attractive leaves; varied habits **Height:** 8–18" for dwarf varieties; up to 10' for trailing varieties **Spread:** equal to or slightly greater than height

Nicotiana
Nicotiana

Nicotiana was originally cultivated for the wonderful fragrance of the flowers, a feature that, in some cases, has been lost in favor of an expanded selection of flower colors. Fragrant varieties are still available.

Growing

Nicotiana grows well in **full sun, light shade** or **partial shade**. The soil should be **fertile, high in organic matter, moist** and **well drained**.

Tips

Nicotiana is popular in beds and borders. The dwarf varieties do well in containers. Tall plants may need staking. Sow seed directly into warm soil, or start them earlier indoors.

Do not plant nicotiana near tomatoes as both are from the same plant family. Nicotiana may attract and harbor diseases that will hardly affect it, but can kill tomatoes.

Recommended

N. **Hummingbird Series** are compact plants with fragrant flowers available in red, pink, lilac, green or white. This series is excellent at the front of a border or when mass planted.

N. langsdorffii bears clusters of bell-shaped, green flowers. The leaves and stems are hairy and feel sticky to the touch.

N. **x *sanderae*** (*N. alata x N. forgetiana*) is a hybrid from which many brightly colored and dwarf cultivars have been developed.

N. sylvestris and *N. x sanderae* Nicki Series (above)
N. x sanderae Nicki Series (below)

N. sylvestris bears white blooms that are fragrant in the evening.

Also called: flowering tobacco
Features: red, pink, green, yellow, white, purple flowers; some are fragrant
Height: 6"–5' **Spread:** 10–24"

Petunia

Petunia

P. milliflora type 'Fantasy' (above), P. multiflora type (below)

Petunias have never been better. Many exciting new types are coming into the market, and improvements are being made to traditional varieties. Look especially for three types at the garden center—Waves, Supertunias and Surfinias.

Growing

Petunias prefer **full sun**. The soil should be of **average to rich fertility, light, sandy** and **well drained**. Pinch halfway back in mid-summer to keep plants bushy and to encourage new growth and flowers.

Tips

Use petunias in beds, borders, containers and hanging baskets.

Recommended

P. x *hybrida* is a large group of popular, sun-loving annuals that can be divided into three categories: **grandifloras** have the largest flowers in the widest range of colors, but they can be damaged by rain; **multifloras** bear more flowers then the grandifloras, but the flowers are smaller and can tolerate adverse weather conditions better; and **millifloras** have the smallest flowers in the narrowest range of colors, but this type is the most prolific and least likely to be damaged by heavy rain.

For speedy growth, prolific blooming and ease of care, petunias are hard to beat.

Features: pink, purple, red, white, yellow, coral, blue, bicolored flowers; versatile plants
Height: 6–18" **Spread:** 12–24" or wider

Portulaca
Portulaca

The reigning champion of the brightest spot in the garden has to be portulaca. It loves the heat, flowers all season, stays in bounds, and it generally doesn't fuss if you forget to water it.

Growing

Portulaca requires **full sun**. The soil should be of **poor fertility, sandy** and **well drained**. To ensure that you will have plants where you want them, start seeds indoors. If you sow directly outdoors, the tiny seeds may get washed away by rain, and the plants will pop up in unexpected places.

Tips

Portulaca is the ideal plant for garden spots that just don't get enough water—under the eaves of the house or in dry, rocky, exposed areas. It is also ideal for people who like baskets hanging from the front porch but who forget to water them. As long as the location is sunny, this plant will do well with minimal care.

Recommended

P. grandiflora forms a bushy mound of succulent foliage. It bears delicate, papery, rose-like flowers profusely all summer. Many cultivars are available, including those that have flowers that stay open on cloudy days.

P. grandiflora (above & below)

Spacing the plants closely together is not a problem; in fact, the intertwining of the plants and colorful flowers creates an interesting and attractive effect.

Also called: moss rose **Features:** red, pink, yellow, white, purple, orange, peach flowers; drought resistant; interesting foliage; easy to grow **Height:** 4–8" **Spread:** 6–12" or wider

Salvia
Salvia

S. farinacea 'Victoria' (above), S. viridis (below)

The attractive and varied forms of salvia have something to offer every style of garden, from cottage to formal.

Growing

All salvia plants prefer **full sun** but tolerate light shade. The soil should be **moist, well drained** and of **average to rich fertility** with lots of **organic matter**.

Tips

Salvias look good grouped in beds, borders and containers. The flowers are long lasting and make good cut flowers for arrangements.

To keep the plants producing flowers, water often and fertilize monthly. Remove spent flowers before they begin to turn brown.

Recommended

S. argentea (silver sage) is grown for its large, fuzzy, silvery leaves. *S. coccinea* (Texas sage) is a bushy, upright plant that bears whorled spikes of white, pink, blue or purple flowers. *S. farinacea* (mealy cup sage, blue sage) has bright blue flowers clustered along stems powdered with silver. Cultivars are available. *S. splendens* (salvia, scarlet sage) is grown for its spikes of bright red, tubular flowers. Recently, cultivars have become available in white, pink, purple or orange. *S. viridis* (*S. horminium*; annual clary sage) is grown for its colorful pink, purple, blue or white bracts, not its flowers.

There are over 900 species of Salvia, from the culinary sage to the many perennial flower species.

Also called: sage **Features:** red, blue, purple, pink, orange, white, bicolored summer flowers; attractive foliage **Height:** 12"–4' **Spread:** 8"–4'

Snapdragon
Antirrhinum

A. majus cultivars (above & below)

With their unique flower shapes, upright stalks that support ever-opening blossoms and wide-ranging color selections, snapdragons remain a popular garden choice.

Growing
Snapdragons prefer **full sun** but tolerate light or partial shade. The soil should be **fertile, rich in organic matter** and **well drained**. These plants prefer a **neutral or alkaline** soil and will not perform as well in acidic soil. Do not cover seeds when sowing because they require light for germination.

To encourage bushy growth, pinch the tips of the young plants. Cut off the flower spikes as they fade to promote further blooming and to prevent the plant from dying back before the end of the season.

Tips
The height of the variety dictates its place in the border—the shortest varieties work well near the front, and the tallest look good in the center or at the back. The dwarf and medium-height varieties can be used in planters. The trailing varieties do well in hanging baskets.

Recommended
There are many cultivars of *A. **majus*** available, generally grouped into four classes: dwarf, medium, giant and trailing. The flowers bloom in summer.

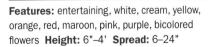

Features: entertaining, white, cream, yellow, orange, red, maroon, pink, purple, bicolored flowers **Height:** 6"–4' **Spread:** 6–24"

Sunflower

Helianthus

H. annuus 'Teddy Bear' (above)
H. annuus cultivar (below)

Birds will flock to the ripening seedheads of your sunflowers, quickly plucking out the tightly packed seeds.

Sunflowers have undergone an amazing transformation. Seek out the new varieties that are more adaptable to the garden and are available in many flower colors and types.

Growing

Sunflower grows best in **full sun**. The soil should be of **average fertility, humus rich, moist** and **well drained**.

The annual sunflower is an excellent plant for children to grow. The seeds are big, easy to handle, and they germinate quickly. The plants grow continually upward, and their progress can be measured until the flower finally appears at the top of the tall plant.

Tips

The lower-growing varieties can be used in beds and borders. The tall varieties are effective at the backs of borders, and they make good screens and temporary hedges. The tallest varieties may need staking.

Recommended

H. annuus (common sunflower) is considered weedy, but many attractive new cultivars have been developed.

Features: yellow, orange, red, brown, cream, bicolored late-summer flowers with brown, purple or rusty red centers; edible seeds
Height: dwarf varieties, 24–36"; giants up to 15' **Spread:** 12–24"

Sweet Alyssum
Lobularia

For years, sweet alyssum has provided literally miles of edging in Illinois, and it will most likely continue to serve that important purpose. Self-seeded plants may pop up in various places late in the season to bid summer a sweet farewell.

Growing

Sweet alyssum prefers **full sun** but tolerates light shade. **Well-drained** soil of **average fertility** is preferred, but poor soil is tolerated. Sweet alyssum may die back a bit during the heat and humidity of summer. Trim it back and water it periodically to encourage new growth and more flowers when the weather cools.

Tips

Sweet alyssum creeps around rock gardens, over rock walls and along the edges of beds. It is an excellent choice for seeding into cracks and crevices of walkways and between patio stones, and once established it readily reseeds. It is also good for filling in spaces between taller plants in borders and mixed containers.

Recommended

L. maritima forms a low, spreading mound of foliage. The entire plant appears to be covered in tiny blossoms when in full flower. Cultivars with flowers in a wide range of colors are available.

L. maritima cultivars (above & below)

Leave alyssum plants out all winter. In spring, remove the previous year's growth to expose self-sown seedlings below.

Features: fragrant, pink, purple, yellow, salmon, white flowers **Height:** 3–12"
Spread: 6–24"

Sweet Potato Vine

Ipomoea

I. batatas 'Blackie' (above), *I. batatas* 'Margarita' (below)

Sweet potato vine has had a gaga response from the gardening industry and should be grown if you haven't tried it yet. This vigorous, rambling plant with lime green, bruised purple or green, pink and cream variegated leaves can make any gardener look like a genius.

Growing

Grow sweet potato vine in **full sun**. Any type of soil will do, but a **light, well-drained** soil of **poor fertility** is preferred.

Tips

Sweet potato vine is a great addition to mixed planters, window boxes and hanging baskets. In a rock garden it will scramble about, and along the top of a retaining wall it will cascade over the edge.

As a bonus, when you pull up your plant at the end of summer, you can eat any tubers (sweet potatoes) that have formed.

Recommended

*I. **batatas*** (sweet potato vine) is a twining climber that is grown for its attractive foliage rather than its flowers. Several cultivars are available. **'Black Heart'** has heart-shaped, dark purple-green foliage with darker veins. **'Blackie'** has dark purple, deeply lobed leaves. **'Margarita'** has heart-shaped, yellow-green foliage. **'Tricolor'** has pink, green and white variegated foliage.

Features: decorative foliage
Height: about 12" **Spread:** up to 10'

Verbena
Verbena

V. bonariensis (above), *V. x hybrida* (below)

Verbenas meet almost every criterion a gardener can demand of a plant. These reliable growers come in a wide array of habits and color combinations.

Growing

Verbenas grow best in **full sun**. The soil should be **fertile** and very **well drained**. Pinch back young plants for bushy growth.

Tips

Use verbenas on rock walls and in beds, borders, rock gardens, containers, hanging baskets and window boxes. They make good substitutes for ivy-leaved geranium where the sun is hot and where a roof overhang keeps the mildew-prone verbenas dry.

Recommended

*V. **bonariensis*** forms a low clump of foliage from which tall, stiff stems emerge, bearing clusters of small, purple flowers. Butterflies love this plant.

*V. **canadensis*** is a low-growing, spreading plant that bears clusters of pink flowers from mid-summer to fall. **'Homestead Purple'** bears dark purple flowers and is mildew resistant.

*V. **x hybrida*** is a bushy plant that may be upright or spreading. It bears clusters of small flowers in a wide range of colors. Cultivars are available.

*V. **pendula*** **Superbena Series** is a vigorous, upright to trailing plant with excellent mildew resistance. The large flowers bloom in intense shades of red, pink and purple.

Also called: garden verbena **Features:** red, pink, purple, blue, yellow, scarlet, silver, peach, white summer flowers; some flowers have white centers **Height:** 4"–5' **Spread:** 10–36"

Vinca

Catharanthus

C. roseus (above & below)

Vinca's adaptability makes it a sure-fire winner. It has cheerful flowers, amazing heat tolerance and the ability to bloom happily despite exposure to exhaust fumes and dust. It is one of the best annuals to use in front of homes and businesses on busy streets.

Growing

Vinca prefers **full sun** but tolerates partial shade. Any **well-drained** soil is fine. This plant tolerates pollution and drought but prefers to be watered regularly. It doesn't like to be too wet or too cold. Plant vinca after the soil has warmed.

Tips

Vinca will do well in the sunniest, warmest part of the garden. Plant it in a bed along an exposed driveway or against the south-facing wall of the house. It can also be used in hanging baskets, in planters and as a temporary groundcover.

Recommended

C. roseus (*Vinca rosea*) forms a mound of strong stems. The flowers are pink, red or white, often with contrasting centers. Many cultivars are available. All-America Selections winners **'Jaio Dark Red'** and **'Jaio Scarlet Eye'** bear abundant red flowers with white eyes.

This plant is a perennial that is grown as an annual. In a bright room, it can be grown as a houseplant.

Also called: Madagascar periwinkle, vinca rosea **Features:** attractive foliage; red, rose, pink, mauve, white flowers, often with contrasting centers; durable plants **Height:** 10–24" **Spread:** usually equal to or greater than height

Viola

Viola

V. x wittrockiana (above), *V. tricolor* (below)

Violas are one of the most popular annuals available. They're often planted in early spring, long before any other annual, because they tolerate frost like no other. Violas require little care.

Growing

Violas prefer **full sun** but tolerate partial shade. The soil should be **fertile**, **moist** and **well drained**. They do best in cool weather, and may die back completely in the summer heat.

Tips

Violas can be used in beds, borders or containers, or mixed with spring-flowering bulbs. The varied color combinations of pansies complement almost every other type of bedding plant.

Plant additional violas in late summer and early fall to refresh faded flowerbeds.

Violas will often re-awaken in spring if left to go dormant in fall, allowing for early-spring flowers. In warmer areas of the state, some pansies will bloom through a mild winter.

Recommended

V. tricolor (Johnny-jump-up) has purple, white and yellow flowers, usually in combination. Several varieties have flowers in a single color, often purple. This plant thrives in gravel.

V. x wittrockiana (pansy) is available in a wide variety of solid, patterned, bicolored or multi-colored flowers with face-like markings in every size imaginable. The bright green foliage is lightly scalloped along the edges.

Features: blue, purple, red, orange, yellow, pink, white, multi-colored flowers; easy to grow; low maintenance **Height:** 3–10" **Spread:** 4–12"

Zinnia

Zinnia

Z. *haageana* 'Orange Star' (above), Z. *elegans* (below)

Zinnias provide lots of colorful flowers on sturdy stems and are a staple in our gardens. They have a wide range of uses in both formal and informal gardens, in containers and as cut flowers.

Mildew can be a problem for zinnias, so choose mildew-resistant cultivars, grow them in locations with good air circulation and avoid wetting the foliage.

Growing

Zinnias grow best in **full sun**. The soil should be **fertile, rich in organic matter, moist** and **well drained**. To avoid disturbing the roots when transplanting seedlings, start seeds in individual peat pots. Deadhead to prolong blooming and to keep plants looking neat.

Tips

Zinnias are useful in beds, borders, containers and cutting gardens. Dwarf selections can be used as edging plants. These plants provide wonderful fall color.

Recommended

Z. elegans is a bushy, upright plant with daisy-like flowers in a variety of forms. Heights vary from 6–36". Many cultivars are available.

Z. haageana (Mexican zinnia) is a bushy plant with narrow leaves and it bears bright, bicolored or tricolored, daisy-like flowers in shades of orange, red, yellow, maroon, brown or gold. Plants grow 12–24" tall. Cultivars are available.

Z. **Profusion Series** are fast-growing, mildew-resistant, compact hybrids. These All-America Selections winners bear bright cherry red, orange or white flowers.

Features: bushy plants; colorful flowers in shades of red, yellow, orange, pink, white, maroon, brown, gold, some are bicolored or tricolored **Height:** 6–36" **Spread:** 12"

Native asters, such as *A. novae-angliae*, decorate our roadsides in fall. Their cultivated counterparts are richer in color, larger in bloom and somewhat better behaved.

Growing

Asters prefer **full sun** but benefit from some afternoon shade to keep them from suffering in August's heat and humidity. The soil should be **fertile, moist** and **well drained**. Pinch or shear these plants back in early summer to promote dense growth and to reduce disease problems. Mulch in winter to protect plants from temperature fluctuations. Divide every two or three years to maintain vigor and control spread.

Tips

Use asters in the middle of borders and in cottage gardens, or naturalize them in wild gardens. The purple and pink flowers nicely contrast with the yellow-flowered perennials common in the late-summer garden.

Recommended

Some aster species have recently been reclassified under the genus *Symphyotrichum*. You may see both names at garden centers.

*A. **novae-angliae*** (Michaelmas daisy, New England aster) is an upright, spreading, clump-forming perennial that bears yellow-centered, purple flowers. Many cultivars are available.

A. novae-angliae (above), *A. novi-belgii* (below)

*A. **novi-belgii*** (Michaelmas daisy, New York aster) is a dense, upright, clump-forming perennial with purple flowers. Many cultivars are available.

Among the final plants to bloom before the snow flies, asters often provide a last meal for migrating butterflies.

Features: red, white, blue, purple, pink late-summer to mid-fall flowers, often with yellow centers **Height:** 7"–5'
Spread: 18–36" **Hardiness:** zones 3–8

Although they appreciate moist soil, astilbes don't like standing water. Use mulch in summer to keep the roots cool and moist.

Astilbes should be divided every three years or so to maintain plant vigor. Root masses may lift out of the soil as they mature. Add a layer of topsoil and mulch, or replant deeper, if this occurs.

Tips

Astilbes can be grown near the edges of bog gardens and ponds, and in woodland gardens and shaded borders.

Recommended

A. x *arendsii* (astilbe, false spirea, Arend's astilbe) is a group of hybrids with many available cultivars.

A. chinensis (Chinese astilbe) is a dense, vigorous perennial that tolerates dry soil better than other astilbe species. Many cultivars are available.

A. simplicifolia **'Sprite'** (star astilbe) is an upright variety that forms spreading clumps. It produces silvery pink blooms and rich green foliage.

A. x *arendsii* cultivars (above)
A. x *arendsii* 'Bressingham Beauty' (below)

With blooms in many pastel colors held above deeply cut, fern-like foliage, astilbes bring a feathery accent to a semi-shady border.

Growing

Astilbes grow best in **light or partial shade** but tolerate full shade, though they will not flower as much. The soil should be **fertile, humus rich, acidic, moist** and **well drained**.

Deadheading will not extend the bloom, so the choice is yours whether to remove the spent blossoms. Astilbes self-seed easily and the flowerheads provide interest well into fall.

Features: attractive foliage; white, pink, purple, peach, red summer flowers
Height: 1–5' **Spread:** 18–36"
Hardiness: zones 3–9

Beebalm
Monarda

Bees and butterflies flock to a garden that has a well-grown stand of beebalm.

Growing

Beebalm grows well in **full sun, partial shade** or **light shade** in **humus-rich, moist, well-drained** soil of **average fertility**. Dry conditions encourage mildew and loss of leaves, so water regularly. Divide every two or three years in spring just as new growth emerges.

In May, cut back some of the stems by half to extend the flowering period and to encourage compact growth. Thinning the stems also helps prevent powdery mildew. If mildew strikes after flowering, cut the plants back to 6" to increase air circulation.

Tips

Use beebalm beside a stream or pond, or in a lightly shaded, well-watered border. It spreads in moist, fertile soils, but roots close to the surface can be removed easily.

Using pesticides can harm or kill visiting insects and prevents you from using beebalm for culinary or medicinal purposes.

Recommended

M. didyma is a bushy, mounding plant that forms a thick clump of stems with red or pink flowers. Many cultivars are available. **'Blaustrump'** ('Blue Stocking')

M. didyma 'Marshall's Delight' (above)
M. didyma (below)

has deep violet-purple flowers. **'Colrain Red'** bears red flowers. **'Gardenview Scarlet'** bears large, scarlet flowers. **'Marshall's Delight'** is mildew resistant and has bright, medium pink flowers. **'Sunset'** bears purple-red flowers.

Also called: bergamot, Oswego tea
Features: fragrant blossoms in shades of red, pink, purple, white **Height:** 2–4'
Spread: 12–24" **Hardiness:** zones 3–8

Bellflower

Campanula

C. persicifolia (above), C. carpatica 'White Clips' (below)

Bellflowers anchor the summer perennial garden. From the mounding varieties to the taller species, there is a bellflower for any part of a border planting.

Over 300 species of Campanula grow throughout the Northern Hemisphere in habitats ranging from high, rocky crags to boggy meadows.

Growing

Bellflowers grow well in **full sun, partial shade** or **light shade**. The soil should be of **average to high fertility** and **well drained**. They appreciate mulch to keep their roots cool and moist in summer and protected in winter, particularly if snow cover is inconsistent.

Deadhead to prolong blooming. Divide bellflowers every few years, in early spring or late summer, to keep plants vigorous and to prevent them from becoming invasive.

Tips

Plant upright and mounding bellflowers in borders and cottage gardens. Use low, spreading and trailing bellflowers in rock gardens and on rock walls. You can also edge beds with the low-growing varieties.

Recommended

Many species, cultivars and hybrids of bellflower are available, with growth habits ranging from low and spreading, to upright, to trailing. The most common bellflower is **C. carpatica** (Carpathian bellflower), a spreading, mounding perennial bearing blue, white or purple flowers. Several cultivars are available. Other popular bellflowers include **C. x 'Birch Hybrid,' C. glomerata** (clustered bellflower) and **C. persicifolia** (peach-leaved bellflower).

Features: blue, white, purple, pink spring, summer or fall flowers; varied growing habits
Height: 4"–5' **Spread:** 12–36"
Hardiness: zones 3–7

Black-Eyed Susan

Rudbeckia

R. fulgida with purple coneflower (above), *R. nitida* 'Herbstsonne' (below)

The cultivar 'Goldsturm' is an excellent anchor perennial because of its long life, bright yellow flowers and long blooming season. It doesn't need division, won't die out in the center and won't encroach on its neighbors.

Growing

Black-eyed Susan grows well in **full sun** or **partial shade**. The soil should be of **average fertility** and **well drained**. Several *Rudbeckia* species are touted as 'claybusters' because they tolerate fairly heavy clay soils. Established plants are drought tolerant, but regular watering is best. Divide in spring or fall, every three to five years.

Tips

Black-eyed Susan is a tough, low-maintenance, long-lived perennial. Plant it wherever you want a casual look. It looks great planted in drifts. Include these native plants in wildflower and natural gardens, beds and borders. Pinching the plants in June will result in shorter, bushier stands.

Recommended

R. fulgida is an upright, spreading plant bearing orange-yellow flowers with brown centers. **Var.** *sullivantii* **'Goldsturm'** bears large, bright, golden yellow flowers.

R. laciniata (cutleaf coneflower) forms a large, open clump. The yellow flowers have green centers.

R. nitida (shining coneflower) **'Herbstsonne'** grows to 7' and has bright golden yellow, ray flowers with a green center.

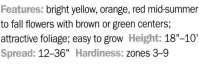

Features: bright yellow, orange, red mid-summer to fall flowers with brown or green centers; attractive foliage; easy to grow **Height:** 18"–10' **Spread:** 12–36" **Hardiness:** zones 3–9

Bluestar
Amsonia

A. hubrichtii (above & below)

Bluestars combine multi-seasonal appeal of spring flowers, solid summer foliage and wonderful fall color. Use them either integrated at the back of a perennial bed or by themselves as specimens.

Be sure to wash your hands thoroughly after handling these plants because some people find the sap irritates their skin.

Growing

Plant bluestars in **full sun to partial shade** in **well-drained** soil of **moderate fertility**. Too rich a soil will result in thin, open growth and not as many flowers. Plants are drought tolerant once established. Divide the plant in spring to propagate more plants.

Tips

These pretty plants have a fine, billowy appearance. Plant in groups of three to five to achieve the most stunning results.

The willow-like foliage of bluestar turns an attractive yellow in fall, and its love of moist soil makes it a beautiful addition to the side of a stream or pond as well as in a border.

Recommended

A. hubrichtii forms a delicate, small shrub with clusters of sky blue blooms in spring. These plants prefer a moist soil. The narrow, feathery foliage turns yellow gold in fall.

A. tabernaemontana produces small, lavender blue flowers. **Var.** *salicifolia* has narrower foliage and more open clusters of flowers than the species.

Also called: willow bluestar **Features:** blue spring through summer flowers; habit; foliage **Height:** 15"–4' **Spread:** 2–5' **Hardiness:** zones 3–9

Bugbane
Cimicifuga

Bugbanes put on an impressive display with long flower stalks held above the dark green, deeply cut foliage. This shade lover is one of the tallest in the perennial border. Fragrance is bugbane's chief attribute, and it continues even after frost in some species.

Growing

Bugbanes grow best in **partial or light shade**. The soil should be **fertile, humus rich** and **moist**. The plants may require support from a peony hoop. The plants spread by rhizomes; small pieces of root can be carefully unearthed and replanted in spring if more plants are desired.

Tips

Bugbanes are attractive additions to an open woodland garden, shaded border or pondside planting. They don't compete well with tree roots or other plants that have vigorous roots. Bugbanes are worth growing close to the house because the late-season flowers are wonderfully fragrant.

C. racemosa (above & below)

Recommended

C. racemosa (black snakeroot) is a clump-forming perennial with long-stemmed spikes of fragrant, creamy white flowers.

C. simplex (Kamchatka bugbane) is a clump-forming perennial with fragrant, bottlebrush-like spikes of flowers. Several cultivars are available, including those with bronze or purple foliage.

C. racemosa is also known as black cohosh, and the rhizomes are used in herbal medicine.

Features: fragrant, white, cream, pink late-summer and fall flowers; some plants have bronze or purple foliage **Height:** 3–8' **Spread:** 24" **Hardiness:** zones 3–8

Chrysanthemum

Chrysanthemum

C. hybrids (above & below)

Chrysanthemums, commonly called mums, fall into the category of 'can't fail,' making them excellent plants for 'brown-thumb' gardeners.

You can deadhead in late fall or early winter, but leave the stems intact to protect the crowns of the plants.

Growing

Chrysanthemums grow best in **full sun** in **fertile, moist, well-drained** soil. Early planting improves their chances of surviving the winter. Pinch plants back in early summer to encourage bushy growth and to increase flower production. Divide plants every two years to keep them growing vigorously.

Tips

Chrysanthemums provide a blaze of color in the fall garden that lasts until the first hard frost. They can be included in borders and planters, or in plantings close to the house. Purchased in fall, they can be added to spots where summer annuals have faded.

Recommended

Chrysanthemum hybrids are sturdy, mound-forming perennials that come in a range of sizes, colors and flower forms. There are many varieties available.

C. **'Mei-Kyo'** bears pale pink to rich pink, double flowers over a long period.

C. **Prophet Series** are popular and commonly available, with flowers blooming in many colors. **'Christine'** has deep salmon pink, double flowers with yellow centers. **'Raquel'** has bright red, double flowers with yellow centers.

Features: orange, yellow, pink, red, purple late-summer or fall flowers; habit
Height: 12–36" **Spread:** 2–4'
Hardiness: zones 5–9

A. canadensis (above), *A. x hybrida* 'McKana Giants' (below)

ew flowers signal spring quite so singularly as columbines. Their nodding flowers and spacious foliage look light and graceful wherever you plant them.

Growing

Columbines grow best with **morning sun** and **afternoon shade**. They prefer soil that is **fertile, moist** and **well drained** but adapt well to most soil conditions. Division is not required but can be done to propagate desirable plants. The divided plants may take a while to recover because columbines dislike having their roots disturbed.

Tips

Use columbines in rock gardens, formal or casual borders and naturalized or woodland gardens.

Recommended

A. canadensis (wild columbine, Canada columbine) is a native plant that is common in woodlands and fields. It bears yellow flowers with red spurs.

A. x hybrida (*A. x cultorum*; hybrid columbine) forms mounds of delicate foliage and has exceptional flowers. Many hybrids have been developed with showy flowers in a wide range of colors.

A. vulgaris (European columbine, common columbine) has been used to develop many hybrids and cultivars with flowers in a variety of colors.

Features: red, yellow, pink, purple, blue, white spring and summer flowers, color of spurs often differs from that of the petals; attractive foliage **Height:** 7–30" **Spread:** 12–24" **Hardiness:** zones 3–8

ral Bells

Leuchera

H. micrantha 'Palace Purple' (above)
H. sanguineum (below)

Coral bells have a strange habit of pushing themselves up out of the soil. Mulch in fall if the plants begin heaving from the ground.

These delicate, woodland plants will enhance your garden with their bright colors, attractive foliage and airy sprays of flowers.

Growing
Coral bells grow best in **light or partial shade**. The foliage colors can bleach out in full sun, and plants grow leggy in full shade. The soil should be of **average to rich fertility, humus rich, neutral to alkaline, moist** and **well drained**. Good air circulation is essential.

Deadhead to prolong the bloom. Every two or three years, coral bells should be dug up and the oldest, woodiest roots and stems removed. Plants may be divided at this time, then replanted with the crown at or just above soil level.

Tips
Use coral bells as edging plants, in clusters and woodland gardens or as groundcovers in low-traffic areas. Combine different foliage types to create an interesting display.

Recommended
There are dozens of beautiful cultivars available with almost limitless variations of foliage markings and colors. *H. micrantha* **'Palace Purple'** started the fascination with darker foliage coral bells when it won the Perennial Plant of the Year in 1991.

Also called: alum root
Features: very decorative foliage; red, pink, white, yellow, purple spring or summer flowers
Height: 1–4' **Spread:** 12–18"
Hardiness: zones 3–9

Daylily
Hemerocallis

With the challenging gardening conditions in the Midwest, we need something that we can count on year after year. There are few garden plants that fit that bill better than daylilies.

Growing

Daylilies grow in any light from **full sun to full shade**. The deeper the shade, the fewer flowers will be produced. The soil should be **fertile, moist** and **well drained**, but these plants adapt to most conditions and are hard to kill once established. Feed in spring and mid-summer for the best flower display. Divide every two or three years to keep plants vigorous and to propagate them. They can, however, be left indefinitely without dividing.

Tips

Plant daylilies alone, or group them in borders, on banks and in ditches to control erosion. They can be naturalized in woodland or meadow gardens. Small varieties are nice in planters.

Deadhead to prolong the blooming period. Be careful when deadheading purple-flowered daylilies because the sap can stain fingers and clothes.

H. 'Dewey Roquemore' (above), H. 'Bonanza' (below)

Recommended

Daylilies come in an almost infinite number of forms, sizes and colors in a range of species, cultivars and hybrids. See your local garden center or daylily grower to find out what's available and most suitable for your garden.

Features: spring and summer flowers in every color except blue and pure white; grass-like foliage **Height:** 1–5' **Spread:** 2–4' or more **Hardiness:** zones 2–9

Euphorbia
Euphorbia

E. polychroma (above & below)

With their bright, sunny, yellow flower bracts that emerge early in the season, their longevity and their easy maintenance, euphorbias are a sure hit. They look doubly lovely come autumn when their foliage turns bright shades of orange, red and purple.

Growing

Euphorbia grows well in **full sun or light shade,** in **moist, well-drained, humus-rich** soil of **average fertility.** These plants are drought tolerant and can be invasive and floppy in fertile soil. They do not tolerate wet conditions. Plant them in spring or fall.

Propagate euphorbia with stem cuttings. Dip the cut ends in hot water to stop the sticky, white sap from running.

Division is rarely required. These plants dislike being disturbed once established.

Tips

Use euphorbia in a mixed or herbaceous border, rock garden or lightly shaded woodland garden.

Recommended

E. amygdaloides '**Purpurea**' (purple wood spurge) has four-season interest—yellow spring flowers and semi-evergreen, smoky purple foliage that deepens as winter approaches.

E. dulcis is compact and upright, bearing yellow-green bracts and dark bronze-green leaves that turn red and orange in fall.

E. polychroma (E. epithimoides) has inconspicuous flowers surrounded by long-lasting, yellow bracts. '**First Blush**' has unique tricolored foliage and rosy flower buds surrounded by yellow bracts.

You may want to wear gloves when handling this plant because the sap contains latex, which can irritate the skin.

Also called: cushion spurge
Features: colorful yellow to orange bracts in spring to mid-summer; fall foliage; low maintenance **Height:** 12–24"
Spread: 12–24" **Hardiness:** zones 4–8

False Sunflower

Heliopsis

False Sunflower is an excellent, long-lived, dependable, back-of-the-border anchor that produces a striking canopy of bright yellow flowers from late summer into fall.

Growing

False sunflowers prefer **full sun** but tolerate partial shade. If grown in an overly rich soil or in partial shade, the plants may need staking during their first year. The soil should be **average to fertile, humus rich, moist** and **well drained**. Most soil conditions are tolerated, including poor, dry soils, but the plants are not drought tolerant over long periods.

Divide every two or so years. Deadhead to prolong the blooming period. Cut plants back once flowering is complete.

Tips

Use false sunflowers at the back or in the middle of perennial or mixed borders. They are easy to grow and are popular with novice gardeners.

Recommended

H. helianthoides forms an upright clump of stems and foliage and bears yellow or orange daisy-like flowers from mid-summer to mid-fall. **'Golden Plume'** has double, yellow flowers. **'Summer Sun'** ('Sommersonne') bears single or semi-double flowers in bright golden yellow. 'Golden Plume' and 'Summer Sun' grow to half the height of the species.

H. helianthoides (above & below)

The stems of false sunflower are stiff, making the blooms useful in fresh arrangements.

Also called: ox eye, orange sunflower
Features: bright yellow to orange flowers; dependable; easy to grow; long lived
Height: 3–6' **Spread:** 18"–4'
Hardiness: zones: 2–9

Goat's Beard

Aruncus

A. dioicus (above & below)

Growing

These plants prefer **partial to full shade**. In deep shade they bear fewer blooms. They tolerate some full sun as long as the soil is kept evenly moist. The soil should be **fertile, moist** and **humus rich**.

Divide in spring or fall. Use a sharp knife or an axe to cut the dense root mass into pieces. Fortunately, these plants rarely need dividing.

Tips

These plants look very natural growing near the sunny entrance or edge of a woodland garden, in a native plant garden or in a large island planting. They may also be used in a border or alongside a stream or pond.

Few plants are as voluminous or grow as tall in a shady border as goat's beard. The nodding, white flower plumes are perfect for late June when spring perennials have passed and before summer blooms arrive.

Recommended

A. aethusifolius (dwarf Korean goat's beard) forms a low-growing, compact mound and bears branched spikes of loosely held, cream flowers.

A. dioicus (giant goat's beard, common goat's beard) forms a large, bushy, shrub-like perennial with large plumes of creamy white flowers. There are several cultivars.

Male and female flowers are produced on separate plants. Male flowers are full and fuzzy, whereas female flowers are more pendulous.

Features: cream to white, early to mid-summer blooms; shrub-like habit; attractive foliage and seedheads **Height:** 6"–6' **Spread:** 1–6' **Hardiness:** zones 3–7

Hardy Geranium

Geranium

Geraniums survive in a wide range of soil and light conditions. Many species grow in full sun in northern portions of the state but prefer afternoon shade in more southern regions.

G. sanguineum var. *striatum* (above)
G. sanguineum (below)

Growing

Hardy geraniums grow well in **full sun, partial shade** or **light shade** in **well-drained** soil of **average fertility**. These plants dislike hot weather. Divide in spring. Shear back spent blooms for a second set of flowers.

Tips

These long-flowering plants are great in a border. They fill in spaces between shrubs and other larger plants and keep the weeds down. They can be included in rock gardens and woodland gardens or mass planted as groundcovers.

Recommended

The Chicago Botanic Garden trial gardens are a good place to see what plant species and cultivars do well in our state. **G. x *oxonianum* 'Rebecca Moss,' G. *sanguineum* 'Elsbeth'** and **G. *sanguineum* var. *striatum*** have all performed well at the CBG. Other geraniums that grow well in Illinois include **G. x *cantabrigiense*** (Cambridge geranium), **G. 'Johnson's Blue,' G. *macrorrhizum*** (bigroot cranesbill), **G. *maculatum*** (wild geranium) and **G. *pratense*** (meadow cranesbill).

If the foliage looks tatty in late summer, prune it back to rejuvenate it.

Also called: cranesbill geranium
Features: white, red, pink, purple, blue summer flowers; attractive, sometimes-fragrant, foliage
Height: 4–36" **Spread:** 12–30"
Hardiness: zones 3–8

Hosta

Hosta

H. sieboldiana 'Elegans' (above)

These shade-loving plants are pretty tough. With great foliage variegation, flowering habits, and even fragrance, hostas rank as one of our favorites.

Growing

Hostas prefer **light or partial shade** but will grow in full shade. Morning sun is preferable to afternoon sun. The soil should ideally be **fertile, moist** and **well drained**, but most soils are tolerated. Hostas are fairly drought tolerant, especially if mulch is used to help retain moisture. Division is not required but can be done every few years in spring or summer to propagate new plants.

Tips

Hostas make wonderful woodland plants and look very attractive when combined with ferns and other fine-textured plants. Hostas work well in mixed borders, particularly when used to hide the leggy lower stems and branches of some shrubs. Hostas' dense growth and thick, shade-providing leaves help suppress weeds.

Recommended

There are hundreds of hosta species, cultivars and hybrids.

Some gardeners think the flowers clash with the foliage, and they remove the flower stems when they first emerge. If you find the flowers unattractive, remove them; it won't harm the plant.

Also called: plantain lily **Features:** decorative foliage; white or purple summer and fall flowers **Height:** 7–36" **Spread:** 2–4' **Hardiness:** zones 3–8

Iris
Iris

Irises come in many shapes, sizes and colors. The most traditional is the tall, bearded iris, commonly called 'flags' in Illinois.

Growing

Irises prefer **full sun** but tolerate very light or dappled shade. The soil should be of **average fertility** and **well drained**. Japanese and Siberian iris prefer a moist but still well-drained soil. Deadhead irises to keep them tidy. Cut back the foliage of Siberian iris in spring.

Divide in late summer or early fall. Replant bearded iris rhizomes with the flat side of the foliage fan facing the garden. Allow tubers to air dry before replanting to help prevent soft rot.

Tips

All irises are popular border plants. Japanese and Siberian iris grow well alongside streams or ponds. Dwarf cultivars look attractive in rock gardens.

Irises can cause severe internal irritation if ingested. Always wash your hands after handling them. Avoid planting irises where children play.

Recommended

Many species and hybrids are available. Among the most popular is bearded iris, often a hybrid of **I. germanica**. It has the widest range of flower colors but is susceptible to iris borer. Several irises are not susceptible, including Japanese iris (**I. ensata**) and Siberian iris (**I. sibirica**). Check with your local garden center to find out what's available.

I. sibirica (above)
I. germanica 'Stepping Out' (below)

Features: spring, summer and, sometimes, fall flowers in many shades of pink, red, purple, blue, white, brown, yellow; attractive foliage
Height: 6"–4' **Spread:** 6"–4'
Hardiness: zones 3–10

Japanese Anemone
Anemone

A. x hybrida (above & below)

Japanese anemones are beautiful plants that bloom at the end of summer when other flowers are fading. They do best in an eastern exposure where they are shaded from late afternoon sun.

Growing

Anemones prefer **partial or light shade** but tolerate full sun with adequate moisture and cooler night temperatures. The soil should be of **average to high fertility, humus rich** and **moist**. While dormant, anemones should have dry soil. Mulch the first winter to help the plants become established. Divide in spring or fall.

Tips

Japanese anemones make beautiful additions to lightly shaded borders, woodland gardens and rock gardens. They look magnificent when planted en masse. Plant them behind shrubby roses to support the tall stems.

Recommended

A. x *hybrida* (anemone) is an upright, suckering hybrid that bears pink or white flowers from late summer to early fall. Many cultivars are available. **'Bressingham Glow'** has deep pink blooms. **'Honorine Jobert'** is quite tall and has plentiful, white flowers with yellow stamens. **'Max Vogel'** has large, pink flowers. **'Pamina'** has pinkish red, double flowers. **'September Charm'** sports rose pink blooms that darken on the inside as they age. **'Whirlwind'** has white, semi-double flowers.

Also called: windflower
Features: pink, red, white flowers; attractive foliage **Height:** 2–5'
Spread: 24" **Hardiness:** zones 3–8

Lady's Mantle
Alchemilla

One of the fun aspects of these enjoyable plants is where you might find them next because they freely self-seed.

Growing

Lady's mantle plants prefer **light or partial shade** with protection from the afternoon sun. They dislike hot locations, and excessive sun will scorch the leaves. The soil should be **fertile, humus rich, moist** and **well drained**. These plants are drought resistant once established.

Leaves can be sheared back in summer if they begin to look tired and heat-stressed. Deadhead to keep plants looking tidy and to prevent excessive reseeding. Division is rarely required.

Tips

Lady's mantles are ideal for grouping under trees in woodland gardens and along border edges, where they soften the bright colors of other plants. They are also attractive in containers.

Recommended

A. **alpina** (alpine lady's mantle) is a low-growing plant with clusters of tiny, yellow flowers that are borne in summer.

A. **mollis** (common lady's mantle) is the most frequently grown species. It forms a mound of soft, rounded foliage, above which are held sprays of frothy-looking, yellowish green flowers.

A. mollis (above & below)

The young leaves of these plants have a mildly bitter flavor and can be added to salads and dips.

Features: yellowish green, early-summer to early-fall flowers; attractive foliage, habit
Height: 3–18" **Spread:** 20–24"
Hardiness: zones 3–7

Lenten Rose

Helleborus

H. orientalis (left & right)

The nodding, cup-shaped flowers of lenten rose are one of the first signs of spring, and the plants should be placed where they can be seen easily. Look for the newer cultivars with double flowers and upright stems.

Growing

Lenten roses prefer **light, dappled shade** in a **sheltered** site. The soil should be **fertile, moist, humus rich, neutral to alkaline** and **well drained**. Protect plants with mulch in winter, though in a mild winter you may find the flowers poking up through the snow in February. Deadheading does not produce new blooms.

The foliage is leathery and the leaf edges are very sharp, so wear gloves and long sleeves when planting or dividing these plants. They don't divide well and usually don't need to be divided. Moving seedlings is an easier method to increase the number of plants. Trim the leaves in spring for fresh growth.

Tips

Use these plants in a sheltered border or rock garden, or naturalize in a woodland garden.

Recommended

H. orientalis (lenten rose) is a clump-forming, evergreen perennial. It bears white or greenish flowers that turn pink as they mature in mid- or late spring.

All parts of this plant are poisonous and may cause intense discomfort if ingested. The sap may aggravate skin on contact.

Features: late-winter to mid-spring flowers in shades of white, green, pink **Height:** 12–24" **Spread:** 12–24" **Hardiness:** zones 4–9

Liatris

Liatris

Liatris is valued for the vertical element it adds to the landscape, for its strong purple color and for its use as a cut flower in fresh arrangements. Although liatris is listed as a sun worshiper, it can flourish in afternoon shade.

Growing

Liatris prefers **full sun**. The soil should be of **average fertility, sandy** and **humus rich**. Water well during the growing season, but don't allow it to stand in water during cool weather. Mulch throughout summer to prevent moisture loss.

Trim off the spent flower spikes to promote a longer blooming period and to keep liatris looking tidy. Divide every three or four years in fall. The clump will appear crowded when it is time to divide.

Tips

Use this plant in borders and meadow plantings. Place it in a location that has good drainage to avoid root rot in winter. Liatris does well in planters.

Recommended

L. spicata is a clump-forming, erect plant. The flowers are pinkish purple or white. Several cultivars are available.

L. spicata 'Kobold' (above), *L. spicata* (below)

Liatris is an excellent plant for attracting butterflies and other wildlife to the garden.

Also called: blazing star, spike gayfeather, gayfeather **Features:** purple or white summer flowers; grass-like foliage **Height:** 24–36" **Spread:** 18–24" **Hardiness:** zones 3–9

Ligularia
Ligularia

L. stenocephala 'The Rocket' (above), L. dentata (below)

Ligularias are stunning plants, but only in areas where they receive adequate moisture and protection from afternoon sun. The foliage and flowers are truly unforgettable.

Growing

Ligularias should be grown in **light or partial shade** with protection from the afternoon sun. The soil should be of **average fertility, humus rich** and **consistently moist**. Division is rarely required but can be done in spring or fall to propagate more plants.

Tips

Plant ligularias alongside a pond or stream. They can also be used in a well-watered border or bog garden, or naturalized in a moist meadow or woodland garden.

Recommended

L. dentata (bigleaf ligularia, golden groundsel) forms a clump of rounded, heart-shaped leaves and bears clusters of orange-yellow, daisy-like flowers. Cultivars are available in varied sizes and colors.

L. przewalskii (Shevalski's ligularia) forms a clump of deeply incised leaves. It produces yellow flowers on long, purple spikes.

L. stenocephala (narrow-spiked ligularia) has toothed foliage and bears bright yellow flowers on dark purple-green spikes. **'The Rocket'** has heart-shaped leaves with ragged-toothed margins and dark leaf veins.

The foliage can wilt in hot sun, even in moist soil. The leaves will revive overnight, but it is best to plant ligularia in a cool, shaded place.

Features: yellow to orange flowers; ornate foliage **Height:** 3–6' **Spread:** 2–5' **Hardiness:** zones 4–8

Meadowsweet
Filipendula

Meadowsweets have the classic look of the prairie—tall, stately plants topped by tiny flowers in airy clusters.

Growing

Meadowsweets prefer **partial or light shade** but tolerate full sun in sufficiently moist soil. The soil should be **fertile, deep, humus rich** and **moist**, except in the case of *F. vulgaris*, which prefers dry soil. Divide in spring or fall.

Tips

Most meadowsweets are excellent plants for bog gardens or wet sites. Grow them alongside streams or in moist meadows. They can also be grown in the back of a border, as long as they are kept well watered. Grow *F. vulgaris* if you can't provide the moisture needed by the other species.

Recommended

F. rubra (queen-of-the-prairie) forms a large, spreading clump and bears clusters of fragrant, pink flowers. Cultivars are available.

F. ulmaria (queen-of-the-meadow) forms a mounding clump and bears creamy white flowers in large clusters. Cultivars are available.

F. vulgaris (dropwort, meadowsweet) is a low-growing species that bears clusters of fragrant, creamy white flowers. Cultivars with double or pink flowers or variegated foliage are available.

Features: white, cream, pink, red late-spring or summer flowers; attractive foliage
Height: 2–8' **Spread:** 18"–4'
Hardiness: zones 3–8

F. *rubra* (above), F. *ulmaria* (below)

Deadhead meadowsweets if you so desire, but the faded seedheads are quite attractive when left in place.

Peony

Paeonia

P. *lactiflora* cultivars (above & below)

Growing

Peonies prefer **full sun** but tolerate some shade. They like **fertile, humus-rich, moist, well-drained** soil with lots of compost. Prepare the soil before introducing the plants. Mulch peonies lightly with compost in spring. Too much fertilizer, particularly nitrogen, causes floppy growth and retards blooming. Divide in fall to propagate plants. Deadhead to keep plants looking tidy. Clean up around peonies in fall to reduce the possibility of disease.

Tips

Peonies look great in a border combined with other early bloomers. Avoid planting peonies under trees, where they have to compete for moisture and nutrients.

Tubers planted too shallowly or, more commonly, too deeply will not flower. The buds or eyes on the tuber should be 1–2" below the soil surface.

Place wire tomato or peony cages around the plants in early spring to support the heavy flowers. The growing foliage will hide the cage.

P eonies have such a strong constitution that their roots with the familiar pink 'eyes' were moved across America with the settlers and became the backbone of perennial gardens for generations.

Recommended

There are hundreds of peonies. Cultivars come in a wide range of colors, may have single or double flowers, and may or may not be fragrant. Visit your local garden center to see what is available.

Features: white, cream white, yellow, pink, red, purple spring and early-summer flowers; attractive foliage **Height:** 24–36" **Spread:** 24–36" **Hardiness:** zones 2–7

Perennial Salvia

Salvia

S. x *sylvestris* 'Blue Queen' (above), *S. azurea* (below)

Perennial salvias are reliable, hardy members of the perennial border. Some of the marginal hardiness salvias that may be perennial in southern parts of the state include **S. guaranitica** 'Black and Blue,' 'Indigo Spires,' 'Argentine Skies,' 'Purple Majesty'; **S. leucantha**; and **S. uliginosa**, a six-footer that grows well in bog conditions.

Growing

Perennial salvia prefers **full sun** but tolerates light shade. The soil should be of **average fertility, humus rich** and **well drained**. The plants are drought tolerant once established.

Deadhead to prolong blooming. Trim plants back in spring to encourage new growth and to keep them tidy. New shoots will sprout from old, woody growth.

Tips

Perennial salvias are attractive plants for the middle or front of the border. They can also be grown in mixed planters.

Recommended

S. azurea var. grandiflora (azure sage) is an open, upright plant that produces azure blue blooms in late summer and into fall. (Zones 5–9)

S. nemorosa (*S.* x *superba*) is a clump-forming, branching plant with gray-green leaves and spikes of blue or purple summer flowers. (Zones 3–7)

S. x sylvestris (violet sage) has grayish green foliage and long-lasting, deep violet blue flower spikes. **'May Night'** bears large, deep blue flowers. (Zones 5–9)

S. verticillata 'Purple Rain' is a low, mounding plant with crinkled foliage that bears light red to violet blooms all summer. (Zones 5–8)

Also called: sage **Features:** attractive, cream, purple, blue, pink flowers; foliage **Height:** 1–4' **Spread:** 18–36" **Hardiness:** zones 4–7

Pinks

Dianthus

D. deltoides (above), *D. plumarius* (below)

The grass-like foliage of pinks adds a contrasting texture in the front of a border. Pinks prefer alkaline soils but need good drainage to flourish.

Growing

Pinks prefer **full sun** but tolerate some light shade. A **well-drained, neutral or alkaline** soil is required. The most important factor in the successful cultivation of pinks is drainage—they hate to stand in water. Mix organic matter and gravel into their area of the flowerbed, if needed, to encourage good drainage. Deadhead to prolong blooming.

Pinks self-seed quite easily. Seedlings may differ from the parent plants, often with new and interesting results.

Tips

Pinks make excellent plants for rock gardens and rock walls, and for edging flower borders and walkways. They can also be used in cutting gardens and even as groundcovers.

Recommended

D. deltoides (maiden pink) forms a mat of foliage and flowers in shades of red.

D. gratianopolitanus (cheddar pink) is long-lived and forms a very dense mat of evergreen, silver gray foliage with sweet-scented flowers mostly in shades of pink.

D. plumarius (cottage pink) is noteworthy for its role in the development of many popular cultivars known collectively as garden pinks. The single, semi-double or fully double flowers are available in many colors.

Features: sometimes-fragrant, pink, red, white, purple spring or summer flowers; attractive foliage **Height:** 2–18" **Spread:** 12–24" **Hardiness:** zones 3–9

Purple Coneflower

Echinacea

This native wildflower has achieved a rarified status among Illinois gardeners. Its vibrant, rich, deep rosy red blooms are among the most attractive in our gardens.

Growing

Purple coneflower grows well in **full sun** or very **light shade**. It tolerates any well-drained soil, but prefers soil of **average to rich fertility**. The thick taproots make this plant drought resistant, but it prefers to have regular water. Divide every four years or so in spring or fall.

Deadhead early in the season to prolong flowering. Later you may wish to leave the flowerheads in place to self-seed and provide winter interest. Pinch plants back or thin out the stems in early summer to encourage bushy growth that is less prone to mildew.

Tips

Use purple coneflowers in meadow gardens and informal borders, either in groups or as single specimens. The dry flowerheads make an interesting feature in fall and winter gardens.

Recommended

E. purpurea is an upright plant covered in prickly hairs. It bears purple flowers with orangy centers. Cultivars are available.

Also called: coneflower, echinacea
Features: purple, pink, white mid-summer to fall flowers with rusty orange centers; persistent seedheads **Height:** 18"–4'
Spread: 12–24" **Hardiness:** zones 3–8

E. purpurea 'Magnus' and 'White Swan' (above)
E. purpurea (below)

Purple coneflower attracts butterflies and other wildlife to the garden, providing pollen, nectar and seeds to the various hungry visitors.

Rose Mallow
Hibiscus

H. moscheutos 'Southern Belle' (above), *H. moscheutos* 'Anne Arundel' (below)

It's always hard to convince people that these outsized beauties are really perennials that deserve a place in the garden. Although the extremely large flowers last only a single day, rose mallow stands up to the abuse of an Illinois summer.

Growing
Grow rose mallow in **full sun**. The soil should be **humus rich, moist** and **well drained**. Rose mallow is a heavy feeder and benefits from a side dressing of fertilizer when it begins to leaf out. Divide in spring.

Prune by one-half in June for bushier, more compact growth. Deadhead to keep the plant tidy. If you cut your rose mallow back in fall, be sure to mark its location because this plant is slow to emerge in spring.

Tips
This plant adds interest to the back of an informal border or in a pondside planting. The large flowers create a bold focal point in late-summer gardens.

Hummingbirds are attracted to these plants.

Recommended
H. moscheutos is a large, vigorous plant with strong stems. The huge flowers can be up to 12" across. Cultivars are available, including some wonderful plants bred right here in Illinois.

Also called: hardy hibiscus
Features: white, red, pink mid-summer to frost flowers **Height:** 18"–8'
Spread: 36" **Hardiness:** zones 4–9

Russian Sage
Perovskia

P. atriplicifolia (above), *P. atriplicifolia* 'Filigran' (below)

The silvery foliage of Russian sage topped by wands of tiny, bluish flowers is sure to catch your attention no matter where it is placed. Its fragrance is an added bonus.

Growing

Russian sage prefers **full sun**. The soil should be **poor to moderately fertile** and **well drained**. Too much water and nitrogen will cause this plant's growth to flop, so do not plant it next to heavy feeders. Russian sage cannot be divided.

In spring, when new growth appears low on the branches, or in fall, cut the plant back hard to about 6–12" to encourage vigorous, bushy growth.

Tips

The silvery foliage and blue flowers work well with other plants in the back of a mixed border and soften the appearance of daylilies. Russian sage can also create a soft screen in a natural garden or on a dry bank.

Recommended

P. atriplicifolia is a loose, upright plant with silvery white, finely divided foliage. The small, lavender blue flowers are loosely held on silvery, branched stems. Cultivars are available.

Features: blue to purple mid-summer to fall flowers; attractive habit; fragrant, gray-green foliage **Height:** 3–4' **Spread:** 3–4'
Hardiness: zones 4–9

Shasta Daisy

Leucanthemum

L. x *superbum* (above & below)

Growing

Shasta daisy grows well in **full sun** or **partial shade**. The soil should be **fertile, moist** and **well drained**. Pinch or trim plants back in spring to encourage compact, bushy growth. Divide every year or two in spring to maintain plant vigor. Fall-planted Shasta daisy may not become established in time to survive winter. Plants can be short-lived in zones 4 and 5.

Deadheading extends the bloom by several weeks. Start seeds indoors in spring or direct sow into warm soil.

Tips

Use Shasta daisy as a single plant or massed in groups. Shorter varieties can be used in many garden settings, and taller varieties may need support if exposed to windy situations. The flowers can be cut for fresh arrangements.

Recommended

L. x *superbum* forms a large clump of dark green leaves and stems. It bears white, daisy flowers with yellow centers all summer, often until first frost. **'Alaska'** bears large flowers and is hardier than the species. **'Becky'** has strong, wind-resistant stems, with blooms lasting up to eight weeks.

S hasta daisy is one of the most popular perennials because it is easy to grow and the blooms are bright, plentiful and work well as cut flowers.

Three years is a good lifespan for most Shasta daisy plants in Illinois because our heavy soil rarely drains well enough to assure winter hardiness.

Features: white early-summer to fall flowers with yellow centers **Height:** 1–4'
Spread: 15–24" **Hardiness:** zones 4–9

Yarrow
Achillea

*Y*arrows are informal, tough plants with a fantastic color range.

Growing

Grow yarrows in **full sun** in **well-drained** soil of **average fertility**—avoid heavy clay. Yarrows tolerate drought and poor soil and abide, but do not thrive in, heavy, wet soil or very humid conditions. Excessively rich soil or too much nitrogen results in weak, floppy growth.

Divide every two or three years in spring to maintain plant vigor. Deadhead to prolong blooming. Once the flowerheads begin to fade, cut them back to the lateral buds. Basal foliage should be left in place over the winter and tidied up in spring.

Tips

Cottage gardens, wildflower gardens and mixed borders are perfect places for these informal plants. They thrive in hot, dry locations where nothing else will grow.

Recommended

Many yarrow species, cultivars and hybrids are available.

A. filipendulina forms a clump of ferny foliage, bears yellow flowers, and has been used to develop several hybrids and cultivars.

A. millefolium (common yarrow) forms a clump of soft, finely divided foliage and bears white flowers. Many cultivars exist in wide range of flower colors.

A. millefolium 'Paprika' (above), *A. filipendulina* (below)

Yarrows make excellent groundcovers. They send up shoots and flowers from a low basal point and may be mowed periodically without excessive damage to the plant. Mower blades should be kept at least 4" high.

Features: white, yellow, red, orange, pink, purple mid-summer to early-fall flowers; attractive foliage; spreading habit **Height:** 7"–4'
Spread: 12–36" **Hardiness:** zones 3–9

Arborvitae

Thuja

T. occidentalis 'Yellow Ribbon' (above)
T. occidentalis (below)

Arborvitaes are found throughout Illinois because of their durability, good looks, adaptation to conditions, range of shapes and, perhaps most importantly, soft needles.

Growing

Arborvitae prefers **full sun**. The soil should be of **average fertility, moist** and **well drained**. These plants enjoy humidity and are often found growing near marshy areas. *T. orientalis,* however, requires good drainage. Arborvitae performs best with some shelter from wind, especially in winter, when the foliage can easily dry out and give the entire plant a rather brown, drab appearance.

Tips

Large varieties of arborvitae make excellent specimen trees, and smaller cultivars can be used in foundation plantings and shrub borders, and as formal or informal hedges.

Recommended

Many diverse cultivars of the following three species are available.

T. occidentalis (eastern arborvitae, eastern white cedar) is a narrow, pyramidal tree with scale-like needles. (Zones 2–7; cultivars may be less cold hardy)

T. orientalis (*Platycladus orientalis;* oriental arborvitae) is a pyramidal to irregular tree with vertical sprays of scale-like foliage. (Zones 5–9)

T. plicata (western arborvitae, western redcedar) is a fast-growing, narrowly pyramidal tree. It maintains good foliage color all winter. (Zones 4–7)

Also called: cedar **Features:** small to large evergreen shrub or tree; foliage; bark; form
Height: 18"–50' **Spread:** 18"–15'
Hardiness: zones 2–9

Barberry
Berberis

Barberries add bold contrast in a shrub border, but it's best to put them in the center of the planting. Effective siting will maximize their visual interest while preventing the decidedly unpleasant experience of walking into them.

Growing

Barberry develops the best fall color when grown in **full sun**, but it tolerates partial shade. Any **well-drained** soil is suitable. This plant tolerates drought and urban conditions but suffers in poorly-drained, wet soil.

Tips

Large barberry plants make great hedges with formidable prickles. They can be very effective for discouraging foot (or dog) traffic from cutting through your yard. Barberry can also be included in shrub and mixed borders. Small cultivars can be grown in rock gardens, in raised beds and along rock walls.

Recommended

B. thunbergii (Japanese barberry) is a dense shrub with a broad, rounded habit. The foliage is bright green and turns shades of orange, red or purple in fall. Yellow spring flowers are followed by glossy red fruit later in summer. Many cultivars have been developed for their variable foliage color, including shades of purple, yellow and variegated varieties.

B. thunbergii 'Helmond Pillar' (above)
B. thunbergii 'Atropurpurea' (below)

B. thunbergii *is being noted as an invasive species in shaded, well-drained natural habitats. Its seeds are typically distributed by birds. The cultivars are less invasive.*

Features: prickly, deciduous shrub; foliage; flowers; fruit **Height:** 2–6' **Spread:** 18"–6' **Hardiness:** zones 4–8

Beech

Fagus

F. grandifolia (above), F. sylvatica (below)

Several magnificent species belong to this genus, but the most impressive specimens are grown in an expansive setting, such as a park, cemetery or woodland. Look for the distinctive, gray, smooth bark in winter.

Growing

Beeches grow equally well in **full sun** or **partial shade**. The soil should be of **average fertility, loamy** and **well drained**, though most well-drained soils are tolerated. American beech suffers in alkaline and poorly drained soils.

American beech doesn't like to have its roots disturbed, so transplant only when very young. European beech transplants easily and is more tolerant of varied soil conditions than is American beech.

Tips

Beeches make excellent specimens. They are also used as shade trees and in woodland gardens. These trees need a lot of space, but the European beech's adaptability to pruning makes it a reasonable choice in a small garden.

Recommended

F. grandifolia (American beech) is a broad-canopied tree native to most of eastern North America.

F. sylvatica (European beech) is a spectacular, broad tree with a number of interesting cultivars. Several are small enough to use in the home garden, from narrow columnar and weeping varieties to varieties with purple or yellow leaves or pink, white and green variegated foliage.

The nuts are edible when roasted.

Features: large, oval, deciduous shade tree; foliage; bark; habit; fall color; fruit
Height: 30–80' **Spread:** 10–65'
Hardiness: zones 4–9

Boxwood
Buxus

Boxwoods define formality in gardens. These versatile evergreens can be pruned to form neat hedges, geometric shapes or fanciful creatures. When allowed to grow naturally, they form attractive, rounded mounds.

B. microphylla var. koreana x B. sempervirens cultivars (above & below)

Growing
Boxwoods prefer **partial shade** but adapt to full shade or to full sun if kept well watered. The soil should be **fertile** and **well drained**. Once established, boxwoods are drought tolerant.

Using mulch benefits these shallow-rooted shrubs. It is best not to disturb the earth around established boxwoods.

Tips
These shrubs make excellent background plants in mixed borders. They are also immune to deer browsing.

Recommended
B. microphylla var. *koreana* (Korean littleleaf boxwood) is quite pest resistant. The foliage turns shades of bronze, yellow or brown in winter. Several cultivars developed from crossing var. *koreana* and *B. sempervirens* exhibit good hardiness and pest resistance. They have attractive year-round foliage. **'Green Mountain'** grows 5' tall. **'Green Velvet'** is shorter at 3'.

B. sinica insularis **'Wintergreen'** is a dense, mounding shrub. It keeps its light green foliage color through winter.

B. **'Wilson'** (NORTHERN CHARM) is a cold-hardy, compact, oval shrub that has delicate, semi-glossy, emerald green foliage with a bluish cast.

Boxwood foliage contains toxic compounds that when ingested can cause severe digestive upset and possibly death.

Features: dense, rounded, evergreen shrub; foliage; slow, even growth **Height:** 2–8' **Spread:** equal to or slightly greater than height **Hardiness:** zones 4–8

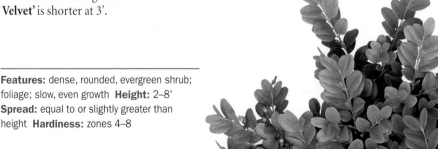

Chokeberry

Aronia

A. melanocarpa cultivar (above), *A. melanocarpa* (below)

All chokeberries offer multi-season interest—abundant white blossoms in spring, showy red or black fruit in summer, and beautiful orange to red leaves in fall.

Growing

Chokeberry grows well in **full sun** or **partial shade**, but the best flowering and fruiting occur in full sun. It grows best in **well-drained** soil of **average fertility**, but adapts to most soils and generally tolerates wet, dry or poor soil.

Up to one-third of the stems, preferably the older ones, can be pruned out annually once flowering is finished.

Tips

Chokeberry is useful in a shrub or mixed border. It also makes an interesting, low-maintenance specimen. Left to its own devices, it will colonize a fairly large area.

Recommended

A. arbutifolia (*Photinia floribunda;* red chokeberry) is an upright, suckering shrub with a rounded top that bears bright red, waxy fruit in fall. **'Brilliantissima'** has brilliant red fall foliage and prefers moist to wet soil.

A. melanocarpa (black chokeberry) is an upright, suckering shrub. It bears dark fruit that ripens in fall and persists through winter. The foliage turns bright red to purplish red in fall. IROQUOIS BEAUTY ('Morton') is a dense, compact shrub.

Features: suckering, deciduous shrub; flowers; fruit; fall foliage **Height:** 3–8' **Spread:** 3–8' **Hardiness:** zones 3–8

Cotoneaster

Cotoneaster

C. apiculatus (above), *C. dammeri* (below)

Cotoneasters come in many shapes and sizes, the most remarkable being the groundcover species that spill into layers of pendulous branches. All cotoneasters have multi-season interest—abundant spring flowers, summer fruit formation and charming orangy red fall color.

Growing

Cotoneasters grow well in **full sun or partial shade**. The soil should be of **average fertility** and **well drained**.

Tips

Cotoneasters can be included in shrub or mixed borders. Low spreaders work well as groundcover and shrubby species can be used to form hedges. Larger species are grown as small specimen trees and some low growers are grafted onto standards and grown as small, weeping trees.

Recommended

There are many cotoneasters to choose from. *C. adpressus* (creeping cotoneaster), *C.* x **'Hessei'** and *C. horizontalis* (rock-spray cotoneaster) are low-growing groundcover plants. *C. apiculatus* (cranberry cotoneaster) and *C. dammeri* (bearberry cotoneaster) are wide-spreading, low, shrubby plants. *C. divaricatus* (spreading cotoneaster) is a rounded to spreading, deciduous shrub with dense, somewhat arched branches.

Features: evergreen or deciduous groundcover, shrub or small tree; foliage; early-summer flowers; persistent fruit; variety of forms **Height:** 6"–6' **Spread:** 2–8' **Hardiness:** zones 4–8

Crabapple
Malus

overwinter in the fruit, leaves or soil at the base of the tree. Clearing away their winter shelter helps keep populations under control.

Tips
Crabapples make excellent specimen plants. Many varieties are quite small, so there is one to suit almost any size of garden, and some are even small enough to grow in large containers. Crabapples are good choices for creating espalier specimens along a wall or fence.

For winter-sapped Illinoisans, few flowers of spring present quite as magnificent a display as a crabapple tree in full array.

Growing
Crabapples prefer **full sun** but tolerate partial shade. The soil should be of **average to rich fertility, moist** and **well drained**. These trees tolerate damp soil.

To prevent the spread of crabapple pests and diseases, clean up all the leaves and fruit that fall off the tree. Many pests

Recommended
There are hundreds of crabapples available. When choosing a species, variety or cultivar, look for disease resistance. Even the most beautiful plant will never look good if ravaged by pests or disease. We in Illinois are very fortunate—the Morton Arboretum is a leader in research on crabapple cultivars.

Features: rounded, mounded or spreading, small to medium, deciduous tree; spring flowers; late-season and winter fruit; fall foliage; habit; bark **Height:** 5–30' **Spread:** 6–30' **Hardiness:** zones 4–8

Dogwood
Cornus

*W*hether your garden is wet, dry, sunny or shaded, there is a dogwood that will suit your planting needs.

Growing
Tree dogwoods grow well in **light shade** or **partial shade**. Shrub dogwoods prefer **full sun** or **partial shade**, with the best stem colors developing in full sun. The soil should be of **average to high fertility, high in organic matter, neutral or slightly acidic** and **well drained**. Shrub dogwoods prefer **moist** soil. *C. sericea* tolerates wet soil.

C. alba 'Bailhalo' (above), *C. kousa* var. *chinensis* (below)

Tips
Use shrub dogwoods in a shrub or mixed border. They look best planted in groups. The tree species make wonderful specimen plants and are small enough to include in most gardens.

Recommended
C. alba (Tatarian dogwood) is a shrub with green stems that turn bright red as winter approaches. (Zones 2–7)

C. alternifolia (pagoda dogwood) is a large, multi-stemmed shrub or a small tree with layered branches and small, white, early-summer flowers. (Zones 3–8)

C. kousa (Kousa dogwood) has interesting bark, early-summer flowers, bright red fruit and red to purple fall foliage. **Var.** *chinensis* (Chinese dogwood) grows more vigorously and has larger flowers. (Zones 5–9)

C. sericea (red-osier dogwood, red-twig dogwood) is a vigorous shrub with bright red stems, small, white flowers and red to orange fall color. (Zones 2–8)

Features: deciduous shrub or small tree; late-spring to early-summer flowers; fall foliage; stem color; fruit; habit **Height:** 5–30' **Spread:** 5–30' **Hardiness:** zones 2–9

Elder

Sambucus

S. *canadensis* (above), S. *racemosa* (below)

Elder fruit attracts birds to the garden.

Elders have what we all want in a shrub—flowers (often fragrant), berries and interesting foliage. However, most elders need pruning to keep them looking tidy. Cultivars with varied leaf characteristics are bringing a new level of awareness to this group of plants.

Growing

Elders grow well in **full sun** or **partial shade** in **moist, well-drained** soil of **average fertility**. Cultivars grown for burgundy or black leaf color develop the best color in full sun, whereas cultivars with yellow leaf color develop the best color in light or partial shade. These plants tolerate dry soil once established.

Tips

Elders can be used in a shrub or mixed border, in a natural woodland garden or next to a pond or other water feature. Plants with interesting or colorful foliage can be used as specimen plants or focal points in the garden.

Recommended

S. *canadensis* (American elder), S. *nigra* (European elder, black elder), S. *racemosa* (European red elder) are rounded shrubs with white or pinkish white flowers followed by red or dark purple berries. Cultivars are available with green, yellow, bronze or purple foliage and deeply divided feathery foliage. S. *canadensis* and S. *nigra* are hardy to zone 4.

Also called: elderberry **Features:** large, bushy, deciduous shrub; early-summer flowers; fruit; foliage **Height:** 5–15' **Spread:** 8–15' **Hardiness:** zones 3–9

Elm

Ulmus

American elms were the classic street trees of Illinois. They created grand archways along many urban and suburban streets. Dutch elm disease dealt a devastating blow to our elms. Fortunately, the Morton Arboretum has become an international leader in breeding resistant varieties.

Growing

Elms grow well in **full sun** or **partial shade**. They adapt to most soil types and conditions but prefer a **moist, fertile** soil. Elms are tolerant of urban conditions, including salt from roadways.

Tips

Elms are attractive where they have plenty of room to grow on large properties and in parks. Smaller species and cultivars make attractive specimen and shade trees.

U. 'Morton' (ACCOLADE; above)
U. americana (below)

Recommended

U. americana (American elm) is a large, long-lived, vase-shaped tree with pendulous branches and shiny, dark green foliage that turns golden yellow in fall. **'New Harmony,' 'Princeton'** and **'Valley Forge'** are disease-resistant cultivars.

Breeding and propagation has produced a number of hybrids that offer good to excellent disease and pest resistance. **'Homestead'** and **'Pioneer'** are hardy to zone 5. **'Morton'** (ACCOLADE), **'Morton Glossy'** (TRIUMPH), **'Morton Red Tip'** (DANADA CHARM), **'Morton Stalwart'** (COMMENDATION) and University of Wisconsin introduction **'Regal'** are hardy to zone 4.

Features: variable, rounded to vase-shaped, deciduous tree; habit; fall color; bark
Height: 10–80' **Spread:** 20–60'
Hardiness: zones 2–9

Euonymus
Euonymus

E. alatus 'Cole's Select' (above), *E. fortunei* 'Emerald 'n' Gold' (below)

Euonymus works well as a background or border plant for stunning fall color and interesting bark, and it also makes a fine specimen as a small tree.

Growing

Euonymus prefers **full sun** but tolerates light or partial shade. Soil of **average to rich fertility** is preferable, but any **moist, well-drained** soil will do.

Tips

E. alatus is used in shrub or mixed borders, as a specimen, in a naturalistic garden or as a hedge. Dwarf cultivars make good informal hedges. *E. fortunei* is grown as a shrub in borders or as a hedge. It is an excellent substitute for boxwood. The trailing habit also makes it useful as a groundcover or climber.

Recommended

E. alatus (burning bush, winged euonymus) is an open, mounding, deciduous shrub with vivid red fall foliage. The corky ridges (wings) that grow on the stems and branches provide winter interest. *E. alatus* has been identified as being invasive in the wilds of Illinois. The cultivars are much less invasive.

E. fortunei (wintercreeper euonymus) is rarely grown in favor of the wide and attractive variety of cultivars. These can be prostrate, climbing or mounding evergreens, often with attractive, variegated foliage.

Features: deciduous and evergreen shrub, small tree, groundcover or climber; foliage; corky stems (*E. alatus*); habit
Height: 18"–20' **Spread:** 18"–20'
Hardiness: zones 3–9

False Cypress
Chamaecyparis

*T*he false cypresses include a number of cultivars that thrive in our climate, and they are diverse enough in form, texture and color to suit almost every garden.

Growing

False cypresses prefer **full sun**. The soil should be **fertile, moist, neutral to acidic** and **well drained**. Alkaline soils are tolerated. In shaded areas, growth may be thin or sparse.

Tips

Tree varieties are used as specimen plants and for hedging. The dwarf and slow-growing cultivars are used in borders and rock gardens and as bonsai. False cypress shrubs can be grown near the house or as evergreen specimens in large containers. False cypress can have survival problems in the northern part of the state due to climate extremes.

Recommended

There are several available species of false cypress and many cultivars. The scaly foliage can be in a drooping or strand form, in fan-like or feathery sprays and may be dark green, bright green or yellow. Plant forms vary too, from mounding or rounded to tall and pyramidal, or narrow with pendulous branches. Check with your local garden center or nursery to see what is available.

C. pisifera 'Filifera Aurea' (above)
C. nootkatensis 'Pendula' (below)

The oils in the foliage of false cypresses may be irritating to sensitive skin.

Features: narrow, pyramidal, evergreen tree or shrub; foliage; habit; cones
Height: 10"–100' **Spread:** 1–55'
Hardiness: zones 4–8

Fothergilla
Fothergilla

F. major (above & below)

Fothergilla flowers have no petals.
The showy parts are the white stamens.

*I*ts honey scent is one of many reasons to grow fothergillas, as are the unique spring flowers, good summer leaf color and vibrant fall hues that hold off until late in the season and include yellow, orange and red, often on the same leaf.

Growing

Fothergillas grow equally well in **full sun** or **partial shade**. In full sun these plants bear the most flowers and have the best fall color. The soil should be of **average fertility, acidic, humus rich, moist** and **well drained**.

Tips

Fothergillas are attractive and useful in shrub or mixed borders, in woodland gardens and when combined with evergreen groundcover.

Recommended

Cultivars are available for both species.

F. gardenii (dwarf fothergilla) is a bushy shrub that bears fragrant, white flowers before the foliage emerges. The foliage turns yellow, orange and red in fall.

F. major (large fothergilla) is a larger, rounded shrub that bears fragrant, white flowers just before, or with, the emerging foliage. The fall colors are yellow, orange and scarlet.

Also called: bottlebrush **Features:** dense, rounded or bushy, deciduous shrub; spring flowers; scent; fall foliage **Height:** 2–10' **Spread:** 2–10' **Hardiness:** zones 4–8

Fringe Tree
Chionanthus

$\mathcal{T}$ree or shrub? Generally grown as multi-stemmed plants, fringe trees tend towards a shrubby appearance but may reach 25' in height—the size of many small trees.

Growing

Fringe trees prefer **full sun** but will grow in **partial shade**. They do best in soil that is **fertile, moist** and **well drained** but adapt to most soil conditions. In the wild, they are often found growing alongside stream banks.

Tips

Fringe trees work well as specimen plants, as part of a border or beside a water feature. Plants begin flowering at a very early age. Both male and female plants must be present for the females to set fruit. Some trees have both male and female flowers.

C. virginicus (above & below)

Recommended

C. retusus (Chinese fringe tree) is a rounded, spreading shrub or small tree with deeply furrowed, peeling bark and erect, fragrant, white flower clusters. It is only hardy to zone 5.

C. virginicus (white fringe tree) is a spreading, small tree or large shrub that bears drooping, fragrant, white flowers.

These small, pollution-tolerant trees are good choices for city gardens. And the dark purplish fruit attracts birds.

Features: rounded or spreading, deciduous, large shrub or small tree; early-summer flowers; fall and winter fruit; bark; habit
Height: 10–25' **Spread:** 10–25'
Hardiness: zones 4–9

Ginkgo

Ginkgo

G. biloba (above & below)

Growing

Ginkgo prefers **full sun**. The soil should be **fertile, sandy** and **well drained**, but this tree adapts to most conditions. It is also tolerant of urban conditions and cold weather.

Tips

Although its growth is very slow, ginkgo eventually becomes a large tree that is best suited as a specimen tree in parks and large gardens. It can be used as a street tree. If you buy an unnamed plant, be sure it has been propagated from cuttings. Seed-grown trees may prove to be female, and the stinky fruit is not something you want dropping on your lawn, driveway or sidewalk.

Recommended

G. biloba is variable in habit. The uniquely fan-shaped leaves can turn an attractive shade of yellow in fall. Several cultivars are available.

There is not a leaf in the tree kingdom that is as distinctive and elegant as the ginkgo's. Even though a ginkgo tree may not have a perfect crown, just getting close enough to discern the fan-like leaves brings joy to tree lovers.

Ginkgo sheds nearly all of its golden fall leaves within a single day, making raking a snap.

Also called: maidenhair tree
Features: conical in youth, variable with age; deciduous tree; summer and fall foliage; habit; fruit; bark; pest free **Height:** 40–100'
Spread: 10–100' or more
Hardiness: zones 3–9

Golden Rain Tree

Koelreutaria

K. paniculata (above & below)

Golden rain tree is one of the few trees with yellow flowers and one of the only trees to flower in mid-summer.

Growing

Golden rain tree grows best in **full sun**. The soil should be **average to fertile, moist** and **well drained**. This tree tolerates heat, drought, wind and air pollution. It also adapts to most pH levels and different soil types.

Tips

Golden rain tree is an excellent shade or specimen tree for small properties. It adapts to a wide range of soils, making it useful in many garden situations. The fruit is not messy and won't stain a patio or deck if planted to shade these areas.

Features: fast-growing, rounded, spreading, deciduous tree; attractive foliage; unique fruit; mid- or late-summer flowers **Height:** 25–40' **Spread:** 6–40' **Hardiness:** zones 5–8

Recommended

K. paniculata is a rounded, spreading tree, 30–40' tall and wide. It bears long clusters of small, yellow flowers in mid-summer, followed by red-tinged, green capsular fruit. The leaves are somewhat lacy in appearance. The foliage may turn bright yellow in fall. **'Fastigiata'** is an upright, columnar tree that reaches 25' in height, with a spread of no more than 6'.

Golden rain tree is not reliably hardy in northern parts of Illinois but should do well downstate.

Hemlock

Tsuga

T. canadensis 'Jeddeloh' (above), *T. canadensis* (below)

Many people would agree that eastern hemlock is one of the most beautiful, graceful evergreen trees in the world. Soft-needled foliage and cinnamon red bark give a distinctive air to the many shape and size combinations of hemlock.

Growing

Hemlock generally grows well in any light from **full sun to full shade**. The soil should be **humus rich, moist** and **well drained**. Hemlock is drought sensitive and grows best in cool, moist conditions. It is sensitive to air pollution and suffers salt damage, so keep hemlock away from roadways.

Tips

This elegant tree, with its delicate needles, is one of the most beautiful evergreens to use as a specimen tree. It can also be trimmed to form an excellent hedge. The smaller cultivars may be included in a shrub or mixed border. Hemlock can be pruned to keep it within bounds or shaped to form a hedge. The many dwarf forms are useful in smaller gardens.

Recommended

T. canadensis (eastern hemlock, Canadian hemlock) is a graceful, narrowly pyramidal tree. Many cultivars are available, including groundcover and pendulous and dwarf forms.

Features: pyramidal or columnar, evergreen tree or shrub; foliage; habit; cones
Height: 5–80' **Spread:** 5–35'
Hardiness: zones 3–8

Holly

Ilex

The wonderful combination of glossy, evergreen foliage and lovely berries puts these shrubs near the top of many gardeners' wish lists. The fact that hollies need to be somewhat pampered doesn't dampen our enthusiasm for them. The deciduous species may be better for northern areas.

Growing

These plants prefer **full sun** but tolerate partial shade. The soil should be of **average to rich fertility, acidic, humus rich** and **moist**. Shelter plants from winter wind to prevent the leaves from drying out. Apply a summer mulch to keep the roots cool and moist.

Tips

Hollies can be used in woodland gardens and in shrub and mixed borders. They can also be shaped into hedges. Inkberry looks much like boxwood and has similar uses in the landscape. Winterberry is good for naturalizing in moist sites.

Recommended

Many holly species, cultivars and hybrids are available.

Good evergreen species include *I. glabra* (inkberry; zones 4–9), *I.* x *meserveae* (meserve holly, blue holly; zones 5–8) and *I. opaca* (American holly; zones 5–9).

Deciduous selections include *I. serrata* (Japanese winterberry; zones 5–7),

I. x meserveae hybrid (above)
I. x meserveae 'Blue Girl' (below)

I. verticillata (winterberry, winterberry holly) and *I. serrata* x *I. verticillata* hybrids (zones 4–9).

Hollies have male and female flowers on separate plants and both must be present for the females to set fruit.

Features: erect or spreading, evergreen or deciduous shrub or tree; glossy, sometimes spiny foliage; fruit; habit **Height:** 3–50'
Spread: 3–40' **Hardiness:** zones 3–9

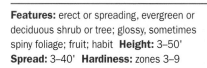

Hornbeam

Carpinus

C. caroliniana (above), *C. betulus* 'Fastigiata' (below)

American hornbeam is a great choice for a home landscape. Its growth is slow and refined (rarely getting out of bounds), and it has interesting, sinewy-looking bark that resembles muscles. The fall color is outstanding, from yellow to reddish purple. European hornbeam is more common in the trade and is good for screening or hedging.

Growing

Hornbeams prefer **full sun** or **partial shade**. The soil should be **average to fertile** and **well drained**. American hornbeam prefers moist soil conditions and grows well near ponds and streams.

Tips

These small- to medium-sized trees can be used as specimens or shade trees in smaller gardens or can be pruned to form hedges. The narrow, upright cultivars are often used to create barriers and windbreaks.

Recommended

C. betulus (European hornbeam) is a pyramidal to rounded tree. The foliage turns bright yellow or orange in fall. Many cultivars are available, including narrow upright and weeping selections.

C. caroliniana (American hornbeam, ironwood, musclewood, bluebeech) is a small, slow-growing tree that is tolerant of shade and city conditions. The foliage turns yellow to red or purple in fall.

Hornbeam leaves remain a bright, fresh green through the oppressive humidity of summer.

Features: pyramidal, deciduous tree; habit; fall color **Height:** 10–70' **Spread:** 10–50'
Hardiness: zones 3–9

Horsechestnut

Aesculus

Horsechestnuts range from trees with immense regal bearing to small but impressive shrubs. All have spectacular flowers.

Growing

Horsechestnuts grow well in **full sun** or **partial shade**. The soil should be **fertile, moist** and **well drained**. These trees dislike drought.

Tips

Horsechestnuts are used as specimen and shade trees. These trees provide heavy shade, which is excellent for cooling buildings, but makes it difficult to grow grass beneath the trees. The roots can break up sidewalks and patios if planted too close.

Smaller, shrubby horsechestnuts grow well near pond plantings and also make interesting specimens. They can form large colonies.

Recommended

A. **x** *carnea* (red horsechestnut) is a dense, rounded to spreading tree that has dark pink flowers. (Zones 4–8)

A. *glabra* (Ohio buckeye) is a rounded tree with a dense canopy. (Zones 3–7)

A. *hippocastanum* (common horse-chestnut) is a large, rounded tree that can branch right to the ground. The white flowers have yellow or pink marks. (Zones 3–7)

A. glabra (above), A. hippocastanum (below)

A. *parviflora* (bottlebrush buckeye) is a spreading, mound-forming, suckering shrub that bears abundant, creamy white flowers. (Zones 4–9)

A. *pavia* (red buckeye) is a low-growing to rounded shrubby tree with cherry red flowers and handsome foliage. It needs consistent moisture. (Zones 4–8)

All parts of Aesculus plants, especially the seeds, are toxic.

Features: rounded or spreading, deciduous tree or shrub; early-summer flowers; foliage; spiny fruit **Height:** 8–80' **Spread:** 8–65' **Hardiness:** zones 3–8

Hydrangea

Hydrangea

H. quercifolia (above)
H. paniculata 'Grandiflora' (below)

Huge blooms and an extended blooming period are two reasons modern gardeners have pushed these old-time favorites back into the limelight.

Growing

Hydrangeas grow well in **full sun** or **partial shade**. *H. arborescens* tolerates heavy shade. Shade or partial shade will reduce leaf and flower scorch in hotter regions. The soil should be of **average to high fertility, humus rich, moist** and **well drained**. These plants perform best in cool, moist conditions.

Tips

Hydrangeas come in many forms and have many uses in the landscape. They can be included in shrub or mixed borders, used as specimens or informal barriers, and planted in groups or containers.

Recommended

H. arborescens (smooth hydrangea) is a rounded shrub that flowers well in shade. Its cultivars bear large clusters of showy, white blossoms.

H. macrophylla (bigleaf hydrangea) is a rounded or mounding shrub that bears pink or blue flowers from mid- to late summer.

H. paniculata (panicle hydrangea) is a spreading to upright large shrub or small tree that bears white flowers. 'Grandiflora' (Peegee hydrangea) is a commonly available cultivar.

H. quercifolia (oakleaf hydrangea) is a mound-forming shrub with attractive, exfoliating bark, large, oak-like leaves that turn bronze to bright red in fall, and conical clusters of sterile and fertile flowers.

Features: deciduous; mounding or spreading shrub or tree; flowers; habit; foliage; bark
Height: 3–25' **Spread:** 3–20'
Hardiness: zones 4–8

Juniper
Juniperus

$\mathcal{F}$ew shrubs are as admired as junipers for their hardiness, adaptability to soil and light conditions, year-round color and tolerance of pruning. A form, color and texture is available for just about any landscaping situation.

Growing

Junipers prefer **full sun** but tolerate light shade. The soil should be of **average fertility** and **well drained**, but junipers tolerate most conditions.

Tips

Junipers make prickly barriers, hedges and windbreaks. They can be used in borders, as specimens or in groups. The low-growing species can be used in rock gardens and as groundcover. For interesting evergreen color, mix the yellow-foliaged junipers with the blue-needled varieties.

Recommended

Junipers vary from species to species and often from cultivar to cultivar within a species. *J. chinensis* (Chinese juniper) is a conical tree or spreading shrub. *J. horizontalis* (creeping juniper) is a prostrate, creeping groundcover. *J. procumbens* (Japanese garden juniper) is a wide-spreading, low shrub. *J. sabina* (savin juniper) is a spreading to erect shrub. *J. scopulorum* (Rocky Mountain juniper) can be upright, rounded, weeping or spreading.

J. virginiana 'Blue Arrow' (above)
J. horizontalis 'Blue Prince' (below)

J. squamata (singleseed juniper) forms a prostrate or low, spreading shrub or a small, upright tree. *J. virginiana* (eastern redcedar) is a durable, upright or wide-spreading tree.

Features: conical or columnar tree, rounded or spreading shrub, prostrate groundcover; evergreen; foliage; variety of color, size and habit **Height:** 4"–70' **Spread:** 1–48'
Hardiness: zones 3–8

The prickly foliage gives some gardeners a rash.

Katsura-Tree

Cercidiphyllum

C. japonicum 'Pendula' (above), C. japonicum (below)

This tree is native to eastern Asia, and the delicate foliage blends well into Japanese-style gardens.

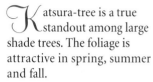

Katsura-tree is a true standout among large shade trees. The foliage is attractive in spring, summer and fall.

Growing

Katsura-tree grows equally well in **full sun** or **partial shade**. The soil should be **fertile, humus rich, neutral to acidic, moist** and **well drained**. Katsura-tree will become established more quickly if watered regularly during dry spells for the first year or two.

Tips

Katsura-tree is useful as a specimen or shade tree. The species is sizable and is best used in large landscapes. The cultivars can be wide-spreading but are more appropriate than the species for smaller gardens.

Recommended

C. japonicum is a slow-growing tree with heart-shaped, blue-green foliage that turns yellow and orange in fall and develops a spicy scent. **'Pendula'** is one of the most elegant weeping trees available. It is usually grafted to a standard, and the mounding, cascading branches give the entire tree the appearance of a waterfall tumbling over rocks.

Features: rounded or spreading, often multi-stemmed, deciduous tree; spring, summer and fall foliage; habit; generally pest free
Height: 10–70' **Spread:** 10–70' or more
Hardiness: zones 4–8

Lilac

Syringa

*O*f you want to get your fill of lilacs in one place, journey to Lombard during their Lilac Festival—Lilacia Park in the center of town is awash in the fragrant blooms.

Growing

Lilacs grow best in **full sun**. The soil should be **fertile, humus rich** and **well drained**. These plants tolerate open, windy locations.

Tips

Include lilacs in a shrub or mixed border or use them to create an informal hedge. Japanese tree lilac can be used as a specimen tree.

Recommended

The following is a short list of really good lilacs. Check with your garden center to see what is available.

S. **x** *hyacinthiflora* (hyacinth-flowered lilac, early-flowering lilac) is a hardy, upright hybrid that spreads as it matures. (Zones 3–7)

S. laciniata (cutleaf lilac) is a dense, rounded shrub that tolerates heat and resists mildew. (Zones 4–8)

S. meyeri (Meyer lilac) is a compact, rounded shrub. (Zones 3–7)

S. microphylla (littleleaf lilac) is an upright, broad-spreading shrub. (Zones 4–8)

S. patula (Manchurian lilac) is a hardy lilac with very few suckers. '**Miss Kim**' is denser in habit.

S. meyeri (above), *S. vulgaris* (below)

S. reticulata (Japanese tree lilac) is a rounded, large shrub or small tree with white flowers. (Zones 3–7)

S. vulgaris (French lilac, common lilac) is a suckering, spreading shrub with an irregular habit.

Features: rounded or suckering, deciduous shrub or small tree; late-spring to mid-summer flowers; habit; easy to grow **Height:** 3–30' **Spread:** 3–30' **Hardiness:** zones 3–8

Linden

Tilia

T. cordata

Lindens have many outstanding attributes that make them fine choices for the home landscape. They cast moderate shade, bear fragrant, yellow flowers in early summer and feature wonderful golden-yellow fall coloring. As a bonus, they even withstand pollution.

Growing

Lindens grow best in **full sun**. The soil should be **average to fertile, moist** and **well drained**. These trees adapt to most pH levels but prefer an **alkaline** soil. *T. cordata* tolerates pollution and urban conditions better than the other lindens listed here.

Tips

Lindens are useful and attractive street trees, shade trees and specimen trees. Their tolerance of pollution and their moderate size make lindens ideal for city gardens.

Recommended

T. americana 'Redmond' is a recommended cultivar of the Morton Arboretum. It has a pyramidal habit, dark green foliage and fragrant, summer flowers.

T. cordata (littleleaf linden) is a dense, pyramidal tree that may become rounded with age. It bears small, fragrant flowers with narrow, yellow-green bracts. Cultivars are available.

T. x *flavescens* (*T.* 'Flavescens') has a straight trunk and a pyramidal to rounded crown.

T. tomentosa (silver linden) has a broad pyramidal or rounded habit and bears small, fragrant flowers and glossy green leaves with fuzzy, silvery undersides. (Zones 4–7)

Features: dense, pyramidal to rounded, deciduous tree; habit; foliage
Height: 20–70' **Spread:** 20–45'
Hardiness: zones 3–7

Magnolia
Magnolia

M. x soulangeana (above), *M. liliiflora* (below)

After a long Illinois winter, the sight of the first star magnolia flowers is sure to lift our spirits. We know, too, that the larger, more languid blooms of the saucer magnolias can't be far behind.

Growing

Magnolias grow well in **full sun** or **partial shade**. The soil should be **fertile, humus rich, acidic, moist** and **well drained**. A summer mulch will help keep the roots cool and the soil moist. *M. virginiana* tolerates wet soil and shade.

Avoid planting magnolias where the morning sun will encourage the blooms to open too early in the season. Cold, wind and rain can damage the blossoms.

Features: upright to spreading, deciduous shrub or tree; flowers; fruit; foliage; habit; bark
Height: 8–40' **Spread:** 5–35'
Hardiness: zones 3–8

Tips

Magnolias are used as specimen trees, and the smaller species can be used in borders.

Recommended

Many species, hybrids and cultivars, in a range of sizes and with differing flowering times and flower colors, are available. Two of the most common are ***M. x soulangeana*** (saucer magnolia), a rounded, spreading, deciduous shrub or tree with pink, purple or white flowers; and ***M. stellata*** (star magnolia), a compact, bushy or spreading, deciduous shrub or small tree with many-petaled, fragrant, white flowers. Check with your local nursery or garden center for other available magnolias.

Maple

Acer

A. *rubrum* (above), A. *palmatum* cultivar (below)

Maples are appreciated for their dense, shade-producing foliage, their neat appearance in a landscape and their near-supernatural coloration in fall. They are hardy, problem-resistant, reliable growers.

Growing

Generally, maples do well in **full sun** or **light shade**, though this varies from species to species. The soil should be **fertile, moist, high in organic matter** and **well drained**.

Tips

Maples can be used as specimen trees, as large elements in shrub or mixed borders or as hedges. Some are useful as understory plants bordering wooded areas; others can be grown in containers on patios or terraces. Few Japanese gardens are without the attractive smaller maples. Almost all maples can be used to create bonsai specimens.

Recommended

Maples are some of the most popular trees used as shade or street trees. Many are very large when fully mature, but there are a few smaller species that are useful in smaller gardens, including **A. campestre** (hedge maple), **A. ginnala** (amur maple), **A. japonicum** (fullmoon maple) and **A. palmatum** (Japanese maple). Check with your local nursery or garden center for availability.

Maple fruits, called samaras, have wings that act like miniature helicopter rotors and help in seed dispersal.

Features: small, multi-stemmed, deciduous tree or large shrub; foliage; bark; winged fruit; fall color; form; flowers **Height:** 6–80' **Spread:** 6–70' **Hardiness:** zones 2–9, varies with the species

Oak
Quercus

Q. bicolor (left & right)

Oaks define the concept of majesty. Their form, foliage, bark and fall color are hard to beat.

Growing

Oaks grow well in **full sun** or **partial shade**. The soil should be **fertile, moist** and **well drained**. Most oaks prefer slightly **acidic** soil but adapt to alkaline conditions. Oaks can be difficult to establish; transplant them only while they are young.

Tips

Oaks are large trees that are best as specimens or for groves in parks and large gardens. Do not disturb or compact the rootzone or ground around the base of an oak; this tree is very sensitive to changes in grade and root disturbance.

Recommended

There are many oaks to choose from. A few popular species are *Q. alba* (white oak), a rounded, spreading tree with peeling bark and purple-red fall color; *Q. bicolor* (swamp white oak), a broad, spreading tree that has peeling bark and orange or red fall color; and *Q. rubra* (red oak), a rounded, spreading tree with fall color ranging from yellow to red-brown. Check with your local nursery or garden center for available cultivars.

Features: large, rounded, spreading, deciduous tree; summer and fall foliage; bark; habit; acorns **Height:** 40–100' **Spread:** 10–100' **Hardiness:** zones 3–9

These stately trees, many of which are native to Illinois, can deliver adaptability, fast growth and a long life span if chosen carefully.

Pine

Pinus

P. ponderosa (above), P. strobus (below)

Growing

Pines grow best in **full sun**. These trees adapt to most **well-drained** soils but do not tolerate polluted urban conditions.

Tips

Pines are more diverse and widely adapted than any other conifers. Pines can be used as specimen trees, as hedges or to create windbreaks. Smaller cultivars can be included in shrub or mixed borders. These trees are not heavy feeders; fertilizing encourages rapid new growth that is weak and susceptible to pest and disease problems.

Recommended

There are many available pines, both trees and shrubby dwarf plants. Check with your local garden center or nursery to find out what is available.

The Austrian pine, *P. nigra*, was often recommended as the most urban-tolerant pine, but overplanting has led to severe disease problems, some of which can kill a tree in a single growing season.

Pines are such a diverse group of plants that it is hard to know how best to recommend them: are they specimens, candidates for hedges or general landscape plants? The answer, of course, is all of the above.

Pines offer exciting possibilities for any garden. Exotic-looking pines are available with soft or stiff needles, needles with yellow bands, trunks with patterned or mother-of-pearl-like bark and varied forms.

Features: upright, columnar or spreading, evergreen tree; foliage; bark; cones; habit
Height: 2–120' **Spread:** 2–50'
Hardiness: zones 2–8

Redbud

Cercis

With its rosy pink cloud of blooms in early spring, redbud is a favorite in almost any home-landscape setting.

Growing

Redbud will grow well in **full sun, partial shade** or **light shade**. The soil should be a **fertile, deep loam** that is **moist** and **well drained**. This plant has tender roots and does not like to be transplanted.

Northern Illinois is close to the northern edge of the range for the native *C. canadensis*, so you may have trouble establishing a young tree if winters are severe. Providing a sheltered location will help.

Tips

Redbud can be used as a specimen tree, in a shrub or mixed border or in a woodland garden.

Select a redbud from a locally grown source. Plants grown from seeds produced in the South are not hardy in the North.

Recommended

C. canadensis (eastern redbud) is a spreading, multi-stemmed tree that bears red, purple or pink flowers. The young foliage is bronze, fading to green over summer and turning bright yellow in fall. Many beautiful cultivars are available.

C. canadensis (above & below)

Redbud can be long-lived if the tree's suckers are allowed to develop and replace the original trunk.

Features: rounded or spreading, multi-stemmed, deciduous tree or shrub; spring flowers; fall foliage **Height:** 20–30' **Spread:** 25–35' **Hardiness:** zones 4–9

Rhododendron • Azalea

Rhododendron

R. 'Purple Gem' (above), azalea hybrid (below)

Rhododendrons are at their flowering peak on exactly the same weekend that we descend like locusts on garden centers in search of anything with color. Carefully consider where the plants will go rather than purchasing impulsively.

Growing

Rhododendrons prefer **partial shade** or **light shade**. Deciduous azaleas perform best in **full sun** or **light shade**. A location **sheltered from strong winds** is preferable.

In a protected location, they should not need burlap covering in winter. The soil should be **fertile, humus rich, acidic, moist** and **well drained**. These plants are sensitive to high pH, drought, salinity and winter injury.

Tips

These plants grow and look better when planted in groups. Use them in shrub or mixed borders, in woodland gardens or in sheltered rock gardens.

Shallow planting with a good mulch is essential, as is excellent drainage. In heavy soils, elevate the crown 1" above soil level when planting to ensure good surface drainage.

Recommended

R. catawbiense (Catawba rhododendron, mountain rosebay) is a large, rounded, evergreen rhododendron with large leaves and clusters of reddish purple flowers.

R. **Northern Lights Hybrids** are broad, rounded, very cold hardy, deciduous azaleas. They are excellent for gardens in northern Illinois.

R. **PJM Hybrids** are compact, rounded, dwarf, weevil-resistant, evergreen rhododendrons bearing flowers in a range of colors.

Features: upright, mounding, rounded, evergreen or deciduous shrub; late-winter to early-summer flowers; foliage; habit
Height: 1–10' **Spread:** 3–10'
Hardiness: zones 4–8

Rose-of-Sharon

Hibiscus

The pros give very clear instructions on the use of this upright shrub: grow it as an informal hedge, or use it in a combined shrub border. Rose-of-Sharon shines in late summer when it brings several interesting colors to the heat-stricken days of July and August.

H. syriacus 'Woodbridge' (above)
H. syriacus 'Red Heart' (below)

Growing

Rose-of-Sharon prefers **full sun**. It tolerates partial shade but becomes leggy and produces fewer flowers. The soil should be **humus rich, moist** and **well drained**. Pinch young plants to encourage bushy growth.

Some cultivars are heavy seeders and can produce unwanted offspring. To avoid this problem, shear off and dispose of the seedheads right after blooming finishes.

Tips

Rose-of-Sharon is best used in shrub or mixed borders. The leaves emerge late in spring and drop early in fall. Plant it with evergreen shrubs to make up for the short period of green.

This plant develops unsightly legs as it matures. Plant low, bushy perennials or shrubs around the base to hide the bare stems.

Recommended

H. syriacus is an erect, multi-stemmed shrub that bears dark pink flowers from mid-summer to fall. It can be trained as a small, single-stemmed tree. Many cultivars are available. Look for the newer cultivars, which elevate this shrub into the realm of horticultural eye candy.

Rose-of-Sharon attracts birds and butterflies but repels deer.

Also called: hardy hibiscus
Features: bushy, upright, deciduous shrub; mid-summer to fall flowers **Height:** 8–12'
Spread: 6–10' **Hardiness:** zones 5–9

Serviceberry
Amelanchier

A. canadensis (above), A. laevis (below)

Serviceberries generally grow with an open habit that gives the feeling of a naturalized plant. They put on a good show of white flowers in spring, and most produce fruit that attracts a wide range of birds. Fall color is another positive attribute, and the tree forms provide good winter interest in their branching patterns.

Growing

Serviceberries grow well in **full sun** or **light shade**. The soil should be **fertile, humus rich, moist** and **well drained**. *A. canadensis* tolerates boggy soil conditions.

Tips

Serviceberries make beautiful specimen plants or even shade trees in small gardens. The shrubbier forms can be grown along the edges of a woodland or in a border. In the wild, these trees are often found near water sources and are beautiful beside ponds or streams.

Recommended

The following species have white flowers, purple fruit and good fall color.

*A. **alnifolia*** (saskatoon serviceberry, alder-leaved serviceberry) is a large, rounded, suckering shrub.

*A. **arborea*** (downy serviceberry, juneberry) is a small, single- or multi-stemmed tree.

*A. **canadensis*** (shadblow serviceberry) is a large, upright, suckering shrub

*A. **x grandiflora*** (apple serviceberry) is a small, spreading, often multi-stemmed tree.

*A. **laevis*** (Allegheny serviceberry) is a native tree with a spreading habit.

Also called: saskatoon, juneberry, shadberry
Features: single- or multi-stemmed, deciduous large shrub or small tree; spring or early-summer flowers; edible fruit; fall color; habit; bark **Height:** 3–30' **Spread:** 3–30'
Hardiness: zones 3–9

Smokebush

Cotinus

C. coggygria 'Royal Purple' (above), *C. coggygria* (below)

The 'smoke' is all an illusion. Smokebush produces inconspicuous yellow flowers in early summer. When the flower stalks mature, long, feather-like hairs emerge and change to pink or purple, giving the effect of puffs of smoke.

Growing

Smokebush grows well in **full sun** or **partial shade**. It prefers soil of **average fertility** that is **moist** and **well drained**. Established plants adapt to dry, sandy soils. Smokebush is very tolerant of alkaline, gravelly soil.

Tips

Smokebush can be used in a shrub or mixed border, as a single specimen or in groups. It is a good choice for a rocky hillside planting.

Recommended

C. coggygria is a bushy, rounded shrub that develops large, puffy plumes of flowers that start out green and gradually turn a pinky gray. The green foliage turns red, orange and yellow in fall. Many cultivars are available. **'Flame'** has purple-pink flowers and bluish green foliage that turns bright orange-red in fall. **'Nordine'** ('Nordine Red') is the hardiest of the purple-leaved cultivars. It has pink flowers, showy red fruit and plum-purple foliage. **'Royal Purple'** (purple smokebush) has purplish red flowers and dark purple foliage.

Features: bushy, rounded, spreading, deciduous tree or shrub; early-summer flowers; summer and fall foliage; easy to grow **Height:** 8–15'
Spread: 8–15' **Hardiness:** zones 4–8

Spirea
Spiraea

S. japonica 'Little Princess' (above), *S. x vanhouttei* (below)

Spireas are old-fashioned shrubs that became cutting-edge choices when dwarf, colorful types were introduced. They are now approaching cutting-edge status again as groundcover species join the mix.

Growing

Spireas prefer **full sun**. To help prevent foliage burn, provide protection from very hot sun. The soil should be **fertile, acidic, moist** and **well drained**.

Tips

Spireas are popular because they adapt to a variety of situations and require only minimal care once established. They are used in shrub or mixed borders, in rock gardens and as informal screens and hedges.

Recommended

Many species and cultivars are available, including the following two very popular selections. **S. japonica** (Japanese spirea) forms a clump of erect stems and bears pink or white flowers. It is parent to a plethora of colorful cultivars. **S. x vanhouttei** (bridal wreath spirea, Vanhoutte spirea) is a dense, bushy shrub with arching branches that bears clusters of white flowers. Check with your local nursery or garden center to see what is available.

Features: round, bushy, deciduous shrub; summer flowers; habit **Height:** 2–10' **Spread:** 2–12' **Hardiness:** zones 3–9

Spruce
Picea

Renowned for their excellent, tall, conical growth habits, trees of the genus *Picea* add an element of formality to the garden. Grow them where they have enough room to spread, then let them branch all the way to the ground.

Growing

Spruce trees grow best in **full sun**, except Dwarf Alberta spruce which prefers **light shade** and a **sheltered location**. The soil should be **deep, well drained** and **neutral to acidic**. Spruces tolerate alkaline soils. They generally don't like hot, dry or polluted conditions. Spruces are best grown from small, young stock as they dislike being transplanted when larger or more mature.

Tips

Spruce trees are used as specimens. The dwarf and slow-growing cultivars can also be used in shrub or mixed borders. These trees look most attractive when allowed to keep their lower branches.

Recommended

Spruce are generally upright pyramidal trees, but cultivars may be low-growing, wide-spreading or even weeping in habit. *P. abies* (Norway spruce), *P. glauca* (white spruce), *P. omorika* (Serbian spruce), *P. pungens* (Colorado spruce) and their cultivars are popular and commonly available.

P. glauca 'Conica' (above)
P. pungens var. *glauca* 'Moerheim' (below)

Oil-based pesticides such as dormant oil can take the blue out of your blue-needled spruces.

Features: conical or columnar, evergreen tree or shrub; foliage; cones; habit **Height:** 3–80' **Spread:** 2–25' **Hardiness:** zones 2–8

Summersweet Clethra
Clethra

C. alnifolia 'Paniculata' (above & below)

Growing
Summersweet clethra grows best in **light or partial shade**. The soil should be **fertile, humus rich, acidic, moist** and **well drained**. This plant tolerates poorly drained, organic soils.

Tips
Although not aggressive, this shrub tends to sucker, forming a colony of stems. Use it in a border or in a woodland garden. The light shade along the edge of a woodland is an ideal location. Try one of the new dwarf cultivars at the front of a border to better enjoy the lovely fragrance.

Recommended
C. alnifolia is a large, rounded, upright, colony-forming shrub with attractive spikes of highly fragrant, white flowers. The foliage turns yellow in fall. **'Hummingbird'** is compact and low growing. **'Paniculata'** produces large flowers with intense fragrance. **'Pink Spires'** ('Rosea') is a large plant that bears pink flowers. **'Ruby Spice'** has deep pink, fade-resistant flowers. **'September Beauty'** bears large, white flowers later in the season than other selections. **'Sixteen Candles'** is a dense, dwarf cultivar.

Summersweet clethra, as its common name suggests, bears wonderfully fragrant flowers in summer. It attracts butterflies and other pollinators and is one of the best shrubs for adding fragrance to your garden.

Also called: sweet pepperbush, sweetspire
Features: rounded, suckering, deciduous shrub; fragrant, summer flowers; attractive habit; colorful fall foliage **Height:** 2–8'
Spread: 2–8' **Hardiness:** zones 3–9

Viburnum
Viburnum

Of you have room for just one shrub in the landscape, make it a viburnum. These attractive shrubs come in many shapes and sizes. Almost all are hardy and easy to care for, with multi-season interest.

Growing

Viburnums grow well in **full sun, partial shade** or **light shade**. The soil should be of **average fertility, moist** and **well drained**. Viburnums tolerate alkaline and acidic soils.

Deadheading keeps these plants looking neat but prevents fruits from forming. Fruiting is better when more than one plant of a species is grown.

Tips

Viburnums can be used in borders and woodland gardens. They are a good choice for plantings near swimming pools.

Recommended

Many species, hybrids and cultivars are available. A few popular ones include *V. carlesii* (Korean spice viburnum), a dense, bushy, rounded, deciduous shrub with white or pink spice-scented flowers; *V. opulus* (European cranberrybush, Guelder-rose), a rounded,

V. plicatum var. *tomentosum* 'Mariesii' (above)
V. plicatum var. *tomentosum* (below)

spreading, deciduous shrub with lacy-looking flower clusters; *V. plicatum* **var.** *tomentosum* (doublefile viburnum), a shrub with a graceful, horizontal branching pattern that gives it a layered effect, and lacy-looking, white flower clusters; and *V. trilobum* (American cranberrybush, highbush cranberry), a dense, rounded shrub with clusters of white flowers followed by edible red fruit.

Features: bushy or spreading, evergreen, semi-evergreen or deciduous shrub; flowers (some fragrant); summer and fall foliage; fruit; habit **Height:** 2–20' **Spread:** 2–15' **Hardiness:** zones 2–9

Weigela
Weigela

W. florida WINE & ROSES ('Alexandra'; above)
W. florida (below)

Weigela earns its way into Illinois gardens because of its striking, long-lasting bloom. The bright, trumpet-shaped flowers attract attention and hummingbirds.

Growing

Weigela prefers **full sun** but tolerates partial shade. For the best leaf color, grow purple-leaved plants in full sun and yellow-leaved plants in partial shade. The soil should be **fertile** and **well drained**. Weigela adapts to most well-drained soils.

Tips

Weigelas can be used in shrub or mixed borders, in open woodland gardens and as informal barrier plantings.

Recommended

W. florida is a spreading shrub with arching branches that bear clusters of dark pink flowers. Many hybrids and cultivars are available, including dwarf varieties, red-, pink- or white-flowered varieties and varieties with purple, bronze or yellow foliage. FRENCH LACE ('Brigela') has lime green to yellow leaf margins. The flowers are dark reddish pink. MIDNIGHT WINE ('Elvera') is a dwarf plant with purple foliage and pink flowers. WINE & ROSES ('Alexandra') has dark purple foliage and vivid pink flowers.

Weigela is one of the longest-blooming shrubs, with the main flush of blooms lasting as long as six weeks. It often re-blooms if sheared lightly after the first flowers fade.

Features: upright or low, spreading, deciduous shrub; late-spring to early-summer flowers; foliage; habit **Height:** 1–9' **Spread:** 2–12' **Hardiness:** zones 3–8

Witch-Hazel

Hamamelis

Witch-hazels are valued for their flowering cycles. Some species and hybrids bloom incredibly early, often in February in years when winter is not overly brutal. Common witchhazel blooms in mid-fall when the accompanying foliage obscures the delicate, yellow flowers.

Growing

Witch-hazels grow best in a **sheltered** spot with **full sun** or **light shade**. The soil should be of **average fertility, neutral to acidic, moist** and **well drained**.

Tips

Witch-hazels work well individually or in groups. They can be used as specimen plants, in shrub or mixed borders or in woodland gardens. As small trees, they are ideal for space-limited gardens.

Recommended

H. x *intermedia* is a vase-shaped, spreading shrub that bears fragrant clusters of yellow, orange or red flowers in early spring. The leaves turn shades of orange, red and bronze in fall. Cultivars with flowers in shades of red, yellow or orange are available.

H. virginiana (above & below)

H. virginiana (common witchhazel) is a large, rounded, spreading shrub or small tree. Yellow fall flowers are often hidden by the foliage that turns yellow at the same time, but this species, native to Illinois, is attractive nonetheless. (Zones 3–8)

The unique flowers have long, narrow, crinkled petals. If the weather gets too cold, the petals roll up, protecting the flowers and extending the flowering season.

Features: spreading, deciduous shrub or small tree; fragrant flowers; summer and fall foliage; habit **Height:** 12–20' **Spread:** 12–20' **Hardiness:** zones 3–9

Yew

Taxus

T. x media 'Green Wave' (above), *T. cuspidata* (below)

Yews are the great forgivers of the evergreen garden. They can be shaped to whatever form you desire—from formal hedges to whimsical topiary figures. Their uses are nearly limitless, their tolerance nearly inexhaustible.

Growing

Yews grow well in any light conditions from **full sun to full shade**. The soil should be **fertile, moist** and **well drained**. Yews dislike very wet soil and soil that is contaminated with road salt. Do not plant them near downspouts or other places where water collects. These trees tolerate windy, dry and polluted conditions.

Tips

Yews can be used in borders or as specimens, hedges, topiaries and groundcover. Male and female flowers are borne on separate plants. Both must be present for the attractive red arils (seed cups) to form.

Recommended

T. cuspidata (Japanese yew) is a slow-growing, broad, columnar or conical tree with dark green foliage. Cultivars are available.

T. x media (English Japanese yew), a cross between *T. baccata* (English yew) and *T. cuspidata* (Japanese yew), has the vigor of the English yew and the cold hardiness of the Japanese yew. It forms a rounded, upright tree or shrub, though the size and form varies among the many cultivars.

Features: evergreen; conical or columnar tree, or bushy or spreading shrub; foliage; habit; red seed cups **Height:** 2–50' **Spread:** 1–30' **Hardiness:** zones 4–7

Carefree Beauty & Abraham Darby

Carefree Beauty (above), Abraham Darby (below)

Carefree Beauty is a magnificent rose that was developed by the late Dr. Griffith J. Buck at Iowa State University. It is one in the long line of Dr. Buck's 'prairie' showstoppers that are perfectly suited to Illinois gardens.

Growing

Carefree Beauty requires a location in **full sun**. **Organically rich, slightly acidic, well-drained** soil is best, but this shrub rose tolerates slight shade and poorer soils.

Tips

This upright shrub's spreading habit makes it an ideal candidate for a low-maintenance hedge. It also makes a fine specimen and will complement other flowering shrubs and perennials in mixed borders.

Recommended

Rosa 'Carefree Beauty' bears small clusters of 4½" wide, semi-double, deep pink blossoms, not once but twice throughout the growing season. The large size of the blossoms compensates for the small number at the end of each stem. The fragrant flowers beautifully complement the smooth, olive green foliage. Orange-red hips add interest from winter until early spring.

Abraham Darby is another fine landscape rose. It bears double, apricot yellow blooms infused with pale pink.

CAREFREE BEAUTY Features: fragrant, large, deep pink blossoms; disease-free foliage; vigorous growth habit **Height:** 5–6' **Spread:** 4–5' **Hardiness:** zones 3–9

Cupcake & Rise 'n' Shine

Cupcake (above), Rise 'n' Shine (below)

Cupcake has strong, healthy growth and blooms throughout the season. It is a disease-resistant, thornless miniature rose that requires very little maintenance.

Growing

Cupcake grows best in **full sun**. The soil should be **fertile, humus rich, slightly acidic, moist** and **well drained**. Deadhead to keep the plants neat and to encourage continuous blooming.

Tips

Miniature roses such as Cupcake are sometimes used as annual bedding plants. As annual or perennial shrubs, they can be included in window boxes, planters and mixed containers. They can be grouped together or planted individually to accentuate specific areas in a bed or border. These roses can also be planted en masse as ground-cover or to create a low hedge.

Recommended

Rosa 'Cupcake' is a compact, bushy shrub with glossy, green foliage that resembles a miniature version of a high-centered, large-flowered modern rose. It produces small clusters of double, pink flowers all summer.

Rise 'n' Shine is a popular miniature selection that works beautifully in containers and along the edges of sunny borders. It bears unusual, quill-like petals in a hybrid tea form in rosette clusters.

CUPCAKE Features: bushy habit; slightly fragrant, early-summer to fall flowers in light to medium pink **Height:** 12–18" **Spread:** 12–14" **Hardiness:** zones 5–8

Double Delight & Just Joey

The aptly named Double Delight pleases with both its strong, sweet, slightly spicy fragrance and its unique flower color.

Growing

Double Delight prefers **full sun** and **fertile, moist, well-drained** soil with at least **5% organic matter** mixed in. This rose can tolerate light breezes, but keep it out of strong winds. This heavy feeder and drinker does not like to share its root space with other plants.

Blackspot can be a problem for Double Delight. Cool, wet weather can promote mildew.

Tips

It's sometimes difficult to find a place in a bed or border for this unique flower color. It best complements solid, deep, dark red or creamy white flowers in mixed beds in monochromatic schemes.

Try planting this rose in a warm, dry location or in a container where it can be easily monitored for disease.

Recommended

Rosa 'Double Delight' is an upright, irregularly branched plant with medium green foliage. The fully double, high-centered, persistently fragrant flowers open cream colored with red edges and gradually darken to solid red. Heat intensifies the color.

Double Delight (above), Just Joey (below)

Just Joey is an amazing hybrid tea rose with fully double, coppery, soft brown blossoms with buff-pink hues. Each petal is lightly serrated and wavy along the edges, resulting in a perfectly rounded form. It has a strong, fruity fragrance.

DOUBLE DELIGHT Features: fragrant, summer to fall flowers in cream with carmine red edges; repeat blooming **Height:** 3–4' **Spread:** 24–36" **Hardiness:** zones 5–9

Flower Carpet

Flower Carpet (above & below)

Since their release in 1991, the Flower Carpet roses have proven themselves to be low-maintenance, blackspot-resistant, long-blooming performers in the landscape.

Growing

Flower Carpet grows best in **full sun**. The soil should be **average to fertile, humus rich, slightly acidic, moist** and **well drained**, but this hardy rose is fairly adaptable.

Tips

Although not true ground-covers, these small shrub roses have dense, spreading habits that are useful for filling in large areas. They can also be used as low hedges or in mixed borders. Their sometimes-long, rangy canes may require pruning to reduce their spread. Flower Carpet roses even grow well near roads, sidewalks and driveways where salt is applied in winter.

Recommended

Rosa 'Flower Carpet' is a bushy, low-growing, spreading plant with shiny, bright green, leathery foliage. It produces single or semi-double flowers in white, yellow, pink, coral, red, or apple blossom, with prominent yellow stamens. The flowers last from early summer through fall to the first heavy frost.

FLOWER CARPET Features: mounding, spreading habit; deep hot pink, white, coral, red, apple blossom, summer through fall flowers **Height:** 30–36" **Spread:** 3–4' **Hardiness:** zones 5–9

Graham Thomas & Evelyn

Well suited to the Illinois landscape, English roses are distinct from other roses. Their delicate exterior often disguises their tough disposition and willingness to thrive.

Growing

Graham Thomas prefers **full sun** but can tolerate slight shade. The soil should be **organically rich, moist** and **well drained**. Deadheading may be required to extend the prolific blooming cycle. Wet weather is no trouble, but do not plant in overly hot areas, because heat reduces flowering and fades the flower color.

Tips

In warm parts of the state, this extremely vigorous rose reaches greater heights if supported, developing into a pillar style or climbing rose. If desired, prune lightly to keep Graham Thomas a little smaller.

Recommended

Rosa **'Graham Thomas'** is a very dense, upright shrub with abundant, light green leaves. It bears beautiful apricot pink buds that open into large, golden yellow blooms that fade gracefully over time. This repeat bloomer begins its first prolific cycle in early summer. There are many other English roses to choose from, ranging in color from pink to antique white, apricot and yellow.

Graham Thomas (above), Evelyn (below)

Evelyn is another stunning English rose that bears huge, fully double flowers in shades of pale apricot. The blooms are muddled in their centers, showcasing the yellow base of each petal.

GRAHAM THOMAS Also called: English Yellow, Graham Stuart Thomas **Features:** strong scented, 4–5" wide flowers in rich, pure yellow; attractive form **Height:** 3 1/2 –7' **Spread:** 4–5' **Hardiness:** zones 5–9

Hansa & Rosa Rugosa

Hansa (above), Blanc Double de Coubert (below)

Hansa, first introduced in 1905, is one of the most durable, long-lived and versatile roses.

Growing

Hansa grows best in **full sun**. The soil should preferably be **average to fertile, humus rich, slightly acidic, moist** and **well drained**, but this durable rose adapts to most soils, from sandy to silty clay. Remove a few of the oldest canes every few years to keep plants blooming vigorously.

Tips

Rugosa roses like Hansa make good additions to mixed borders and beds and can also be used as hedges or specimens. They are often used on steep banks to prevent soil erosion. Their prickly branches deter people from walking across flower beds and compacting the soil.

Recommended

Rosa 'Hansa' is a bushy shrub with arching canes and leathery, deeply veined, bright green leaves. The double flowers are produced all summer. The bright orange hips persist into winter. Other rugosa roses include **'Blanc Double de Coubert,'** which produces white, double flowers all summer.

Rosa rugosa is a wide-spreading plant with disease-resistant foliage, a trait it has passed on to many hybrids and cultivars.

HANSA Features: dense, arching habit; clove-scented, mauve purple or mauve red early-summer to fall flowers; orange-red hips
Height: 4–5' **Spread:** 5–6'
Hardiness: zones 3–8

Iceberg

Iceberg (above & below)

Over 40 years have passed since this exceptional rose was first introduced, and its dainty, continuous blooms are still popular today.

Growing

Iceberg grows best in **full sun**. The soil should be **fertile, humus rich, slightly acidic, moist** and **well drained**. Winter protection is required. Deadhead to prolong blooming.

Tips

Iceberg is a popular addition to mixed borders and beds, and it also works well as a specimen. Plant it in a well-used area or near a window where its flower fragrance can best be enjoyed. This rose can also be included in large planters or patio containers.

Recommended

Rosa **'Iceberg'** is a vigorous shrub with a rounded, bushy habit and light green foliage. It produces clusters of semi-double flowers in several flushes from early summer to fall. A climbing variation of this rose is reputed to be the best climbing white rose ever developed.

ICEBERG Also called: Fée des Neiges **Features:** bushy habit; strong, sweet fragrance; early-summer to fall flowers in white, sometimes flushed with pink during cool or wet weather **Height:** 3–4' **Spread:** 3–4' **Hardiness:** zones 5–8

Knock Out & The Fairy

Knock Out (above), The Fairy (below)

The Knock Out series, bred by Wisconsinite Bill Radler, brings a whole new level to shrub roses through toughness, disease resistance and its near-continuous blooming. It has been called "perhaps the best-ever landscape rose for four-season interest."

Growing

Knock Out grows best in **full sun**. The soil should be **fertile, humus rich, slightly acidic, moist** and **well drained**. This rose blooms most prolifically in warm weather but has deeper red flowers in cooler weather. Deadhead lightly to keep the plant tidy and to encourage prolific blooming.

Tips

This vigorous rose makes a beautiful specimen plant in a mixed bed or border and is attractive when planted in groups of three or more.

Recommended

Rosa 'Knock Out' has a rounded form with glossy, green leaves that turn to shades of burgundy in fall. The bright, cherry red flowers are borne almost all summer and in early fall. Orange-red hips last well into winter. Available cultivars include a light pink selection called '**Blushing Knock Out**,' as well as '**Double Knock Out**' and '**Pink Knock Out**.' All have excellent disease resistance.

The Fairy is another well-known modern shrub rose. It can be used as a ground-cover or left to trail over a low wall or embankment.

KNOCK OUT Features: rounded habit; light, tea rose–scented, mid-summer to fall flowers in shades of pink and red; disease resistant **Height:** 3–4' **Spread:** 3–4' **Hardiness:** zones 4–10

New Dawn & Handel

New Dawn (above), Handel (below)

*I*ntroduced in 1930, New Dawn is still a favorite climbing rose of gardeners and rosarians alike.

Growing

New Dawn grows best in **full sun**. The soil should be **average to fertile, humus rich, slightly acidic, moist** and **well drained**. This rose is disease resistant.

Tips

Train New Dawn to climb pergolas, walls, pillars, arbors, trellises and fences. With some judicious pruning, this rose can be trained to form a bushy shrub or hedge. Plant it where the summer-long profusion of blooms will welcome visitors to your home.

Recommended

Rosa 'New Dawn' is a vigorous climber with upright, arching canes and glossy, green foliage. It bears pale pink flowers (singly or in small clusters).

Handel is another climbing rose that loves the heat. It bears semi-double, white to creamy blossoms edged in deep pink.

NEW DAWN Features: glossy, green foliage; climbing habit; long blooming period; pale pearl pink flowers with a sweet, apple-like fragrance **Height:** 10–15' **Spread:** 10–15' **Hardiness:** zones 4–9

Old Blush *&* Belle Amour

Old Blush (above), Belle Amour (below)

Old Blush was one of four roses that were brought to Europe from China in the mid-1700s. It was used to create many of the modern repeat bloom roses that are so popular today.

Growing

Old Blush grows well in **full sun** or **partial shade**. The soil should be **fertile, humus rich** and **well drained**.

Tips

This small rose bush looks stunning at the front of a mixed shrub border or within a rose garden. The blossoms have a sweet pea scent and are best enjoyed near pathways, balconies, patios and windows.

Recommended

Rosa 'Old Blush' is an upright, bushy shrub with a moderately vigorous growth habit. This China rose is resistant to disease and produces smooth canes with few thorns. The smooth, glossy leaves are abundant. Semi-double to double, medium pink blossoms are produced continually from summer to winter.

Belle Amour is another old garden rose selection that is sure to please.

OLD BLUSH Also called: Common Blush China, Monthly Rose, Parson's Pink China **Features:** lightly fragrant, pink flowers; disease resistant **Height:** 3–4' **Spread:** 36" **Hardiness:** zones 7–9

Queen Elizabeth

The grandiflora classification was originally created to accommodate this rose. Queen Elizabeth is one of the most widely grown and best-loved roses.

Growing

Queen Elizabeth grows best in **full sun**. The soil should be **average to fertile, humus rich, slightly acidic, moist** and **well drained**, but this durable rose adapts to most soils and tolerates high heat and humidity. Each spring, prune the plants back to 5–7 canes each with 5–7 buds.

Tips

Queen Elizabeth is a trouble-free rose that makes a good addition to mixed borders and beds. It can also be grown as a specimen, to form a hedge or in a large planter. Its flowers are borne on sturdy stems that make them useful for floral arrangements.

Recommended

Rosa 'Queen Elizabeth' is a bushy shrub with glossy, dark green foliage and dark stems. The cup-shaped, double, pink flowers may be borne singly or in small clusters.

Queen Elizabeth (above & below)

Queen Elizabeth has won many honors and was named World's Favorite Rose in 1979.

QUEEN ELIZABETH Features: glossy, dark green, disease-resistant foliage; lightly scented, soft, pearly pink flowers from summer to fall **Height:** 4–6' **Spread:** 30–36" **Hardiness:** zones 5–9

Akebia
Akebia

A. quinata (above & below)

This vine can quickly provide privacy and shade when grown over a chain-link fence or on a trellis next to a porch.

Fiveleaf akebia has lacy, blue-green foliage that masks this vine's penchant for being rambunctious. Small, fragrant flowers of chocolate purple are followed by long seed pods.

Growing
Akebia grows equally well in **full sun**, **light shade** or **partial shade** in **well-drained** soil of **average to high fertility**. It tolerates dry or moist soils and full shade.

Tips
Although the flowers and fruit of this twining vine are interesting, it is worth growing for the foliage alone. Akebia will quickly cover any sturdy structure such as a porch railing, trellis, pergola, arbor or fence. Cut the plant back as much and as often as needed to keep it under control. Akebia plants are deer resistant.

Recommended
A. quinata is a fast-growing, twining, deciduous climbing vine. The new foliage is tinged purple in the spring and matures to an attractive blue-green. Deep purple flowers are borne in spring, followed by sausage-like fruit pods. **'Fruitful Combo'** is the combination of *A. quinata* and its cultivar **'Alba'** in the same container. They cross-pollinate to provide large, showy, colorful fruit.

Also called: fiveleaf akebia
Features: foliage; habit; purple flowers; fruit
Height: 20–40' **Spread:** 20–40'
Hardiness: zones 4–8

Chinese Wisteria
Wisteria

*L*oose clusters of purple hang like lace from the branches of wisteria. With prudent pruning, a gardener can create beautiful tree forms and attractive arbor specimens.

Growing

Wisterias grow well in **full sun** or **partial shade**, though blooming may be reduced in partial shade. The soil should be of **average fertility, moist** and **well drained**. Too fertile a soil will produce lots of vegetative growth but very few flowers. Avoid planting wisteria near a lawn where fertilizer may leach over to your vine.

Tips

These vines require something to twine around, such as an arbor or other sturdy structure. Select a permanent site; wisterias don't like to be moved. They may send up suckers and can root wherever the branches touch the ground. All parts of these plants are poisonous.

Recommended

W. sinensis (Chinese wisteria) is a twining, woody, deciduous vine that bears long, pendant clusters of fragrant, blue-purple flowers in late spring. The medium green foliage can be tinged bronze when new. **'Alba'** has white flowers.

W. sinensis (above & below)

To keep wisteria blooming sporadically all summer, prune off flowering spikes as soon as the flowers fade. A long-handled pole pruner works well. Wisteria will send out new blooming shoots until frost.

Features: blue, purple, pink, white late-spring flowers; attractive foliage; twining habit
Height: 20–30' or more **Spread:** 20–30' or more **Hardiness:** zones 4–8

Clematis

Clematis

C. 'Etoile Violette' (above)
C. 'Gravetye Beauty' (below)

Growing

Clematis plants prefer **full sun** but tolerate partial shade. The soil should be **fertile, humus rich, moist** and **well drained**. They enjoy warm, sunny weather but prefer to have cool roots. A thick layer of mulch or a planting of low, shade-providing perennials will protect the tender roots. Clematis are quite cold hardy but fare best when protected from winter wind. The rootball should be planted about 2" beneath the soil surface.

Tips

Clematis vines can climb up structures such as trellises, railings, fences and arbors. They can also be allowed to grow over shrubs and up trees and can be used as groundcover.

Recommended

There are many species, hybrids and cultivars of clematis. The flower forms, blooming times and sizes of the plants can vary. ***C. maximowicziana*** (*C. terniflora*; sweet autumn clematis) produces tiny, cream white, sweetly scented blooms. For containers, look for the **Raymond Evison Patio Clematis Collection**; most varieties grow 24-36" in height.

Clematis is one of the most rewarding plants that can possibly be grown in a home garden. There are so many species, hybrids and cultivars of clematis that it is possible to have one in bloom all season.

Also called: virgin's bower
Features: twining habit; blue, purple, pink, yellow, red, white early to late-summer flowers; decorative seedheads **Height:** 8–30'
Spread: 2–4' **Hardiness:** zones 4–8

Climbing Hydrangea

Hydrangea

H. anomala subsp. *petiolaris* (above & below)

A mature climbing hydrangea can cover an entire wall, and with its dark, glossy leaves and delicate, lacy flowers, it is quite possibly one of the most stunning climbing plants available.

Growing

Climbing hydrangeas grow well in **full sun** or **partial shade**. Light or partial shade will reduce leaf and flower scorch in the hotter regions. The soil should be of **average to high fertility, humus rich, moist** and **well drained**. These plants perform best in cool, moist conditions.

Tips

Climbing hydrangea climbs up trees, walls, fences, pergolas and arbors. It clings to walls by means of aerial roots, so it needs no support, just a somewhat textured surface. It also grows over rocks, can be used as a groundcover and can be trained to form a small tree or shrub.

Recommended

H. anomala **subsp.** *petiolaris* (*H. petiolaris*) is a clinging vine with dark, glossy green leaves that sometimes turn an attractive yellow in fall. For more than a month in mid-summer, the vine is covered with white, lacy-looking flowers, and the entire plant appears to be veiled in a lacy mist. These plants produce the most flowers when exposed to some direct sunlight each day.

Features: white flowers; clinging habit; exfoliating bark **Height:** 50–80'
Spread: 50–80' **Hardiness:** zones 4–9

Hardy Kiwi
Actinidia

A. kolomikta (above), *A. arguta* (below)

Both a male and a female vine must be present for fruit to be produced. The plants are often sold in pairs.

Hardy kiwi is a handsome and hardy vine. Its lush green leaves, vigor and adaptability make it very useful, especially on difficult sites.

Growing
Hardy kiwi vines grow best in **full sun**. The soil should be **fertile** and **well drained**. These plants require shelter from strong winds.

Tips
Hardy kiwis need a sturdy structure to twine around. Pergolas, arbors and sufficiently large and sturdy fences provide good support. Given a trellis against a wall, a tree or some other upright structure, hardy kiwis will twine upward all summer. They can also be grown in containers.

Hardy kiwi vines can grow uncontrollably. Don't be afraid to prune them back if they are getting out of hand.

Recommended
There are two hardy kiwi vines commonly grown in Illinois gardens. *A. arguta* (hardy kiwi, bower actinidia) has dark green, heart-shaped leaves, white flowers and smooth-skinned, greenish yellow, edible fruit. *A. kolomikta* (variegated kiwi vine, kolomikta actinidia) has green leaves strongly variegated with white and pink, white flowers and smooth-skinned, greenish yellow, edible fruit.

Features: white early-summer flowers; edible fruit; twining habit **Height:** 15–30'
Spread: 15–30' **Hardiness:** zones 3–8

Honeysuckle

Lonicera

Climbing honeysuckles typically feature intricate, fragrant flowers of multiple colors. They bloom over a long period and can set fruit towards autumn. The fragrant flowers attract hummingbirds as well as bees and other pollinating insects.

Growing

Honeysuckles grow well in **full sun** or **partial shade**. The soil should be **average to fertile, humus rich, moist** and **well drained**.

Tips

Honeysuckle vines are twining, deciduous climbers that can be trained to grow up a trellis, fence, arbor or other structure. They can spread as widely as they climb to fill the space provided.

Recommended

L. x *heckrottii* (goldflame honeysuckle) is a deciduous to semi-evergreen vine with attractive blue-green foliage. It bears fragrant, pink and yellow flowers.

L. 'John Clayton' is a compact, floriferous selection with attractive blue-green foliage, large, fragrant, soft-yellow to golden yellow flowers, and profuse orange-red fall berries.

L. periclymenum (common honeysuckle, woodbine) bears fragrant, red- or purple-flushed, white or yellow flowers.

L. sempervirens (trumpet honeysuckle, coral honeysuckle) bears orange or red flowers. Many cultivars are available with flowers in yellow, red or scarlet. It is hardy to zone 5.

Features: pink, yellow, white spring, summer or fall flowers; twining habit; fruit
Height: 6–20' **Spread:** 6–20'
Hardiness: zones 4–8

L. sempervirens (above), *L.* x *heckrottii* (below)

Choosing the right honeysuckle, planting it in the proper site and pruning regularly make all the difference in enjoying these plants.

Hyacinth Bean
Lablab (Dolichos)

L. purpureus (above & below)

Think of hyacinth beans as sweet peas on steroids. The vines grow profusely, providing great visual interest, including the iridescent purple seed pods that, when cooked carefully, can double as a food crop.

Growing

Hyacinth bean prefers **full sun**. The soil should be **average to fertile, moist** and **well drained**. Feed it regularly to encourage plentiful flowering. Direct sow seeds around the last-frost date, or start indoors in peat pots in early spring.

Tips

Hyacinth bean needs a trellis, net, pole or other structure to twine up. Plant it against a fence or near a balcony. If you grow it as a groundcover, make sure it doesn't engulf smaller plants.

Recommended

L. purpureus (*Dolichos lablab*) is a vigorously twining vine. It can grow up to 30' tall, but when grown as an annual, it grows about 10–15' tall. It bears many purple or white flowers over summer, followed by deep purple pods.

Also called: Egyptian bean, lablab bean, lablab, Indian bean **Features:** large, bold leaves; habit; sweet-pea–like, purple or white flowers; purple seed pods
Height: 10–15' **Spread:** variable
Hardiness: grown as an annual

Morning Glory
Ipomoea

Morning glories are fast growing and floriferous. Once their cup-shaped blooms open, butterflies and hummingbirds feed on them.

Growing

Morning glory grows best in **full sun** in **light, well-drained** soil of **poor fertility** but tolerates any type of soil. Soak seeds for 24 hours before sowing. Start seeds in individual peat pots if sowing indoors. Plant in late spring.

Tips

Morning glory can be grown anywhere: on fences, walls, trees, trellises or arbors. As a groundcover, it will cover any obstacle it encounters.

This vine must twine around objects, such as wire or cord, in order to climb. However, wide fence posts, walls or other broad objects are too large.

Recommended

I. alba (moonflower) has sweetly scented, white flowers that open at night.

I. lobata (mina lobata, firecracker vine, exotic love) has red buds and orange flowers that mature to yellow, giving the flower spike a fire-like appearance.

I. tricolor (morning glory) produces purple or blue flowers with white centers. Many cultivars are available. **'Good Morning Red'** is a very compact, 10–12" tall selection from **Simply Beautiful**. It has variegated, creamy white and green leaves and red picotee flowers with white edges.

Features: fast growth; white, blue, yellow, red, pink, purple, variegated flowers
Height: 10–12' **Spread:** 12–24"
Hardiness: annual

I. alba (above), *I. tricolor* (below)

Each morning glory flower lasts for only one day. The buds form a spiral that slowly unfurls as the day brightens with the rising sun.

Sweet Pea

Lathyrus

L. odoratus cultivars (above & below)

$\mathcal{A}$ vine with colorful flowers that smells wonderful as well. Who could ask for more?

Growing

Sweet peas prefer **full sun** but tolerate light shade. The soil should be **fertile, high in organic matter, moist** and **well drained**. The plants tolerate light frost. Fertilize very lightly during flowering season. Deadhead all blooms.

Soak seeds in water for 24 hours or nick them with a nail file before planting. Plant seeds early, as sweet peas can stall and die off as the temperatures rise. Provide mulch to keep the roots cool. Plant a second crop about a month after the first one for a longer blooming period.

Tips

Sweet peas will grow up poles, trellises and fences or over rocks. They cling by wrapping tendrils around whatever they are growing up, so they do best when they have a rough surface, chain-link fence, small twigs or a net to cling to.

Recommended

There are many cultivars of **L. odoratus**, including some that are small and bushy rather than climbing. Heritage varieties are often the most fragrant. **'Bouquet Mix'** bears large flowers in a wide color range. The long, heavy stems make it great for cutting.

Avoid planting sweet peas in the same location two years in a row to help prevent some diseases from occurring.

Features: clinging habit; pink, red, purple, lavender, blue, salmon, pale yellow, peach, white, bicolored summer flowers
Height: 1–6' **Spread:** 6–12"
Hardiness: hardy annual

Virginia Creeper • Boston Ivy

Parthenocissus

These vigorous vines are often mistaken for ivy and indeed behave like many of the true ivies (*Hedera*). They can cling to nearly any vertical surface or can be grown as groundcovers.

Growing

These vines grow well in any light from **full sun to full shade**. The soil should be **fertile** and **well drained**. The plants will adapt to clay or sandy soils.

Tips

Virginia creeper and Boston ivy are woody, deciduous vines that can cover an entire building, given enough time. They do not require support because they have clinging rootlets that can adhere to just about any surface, even smooth wood, vinyl or metal. Give the plants a lot of space and let them cover a wall, fence or arbor. When used as groundcovers, they will spread 50' but will be only 12" tall.

Recommended

P. quinquefolia (Virginia creeper, woodbine) has dark green foliage. Each leaf, divided into five leaflets, turns flame red in fall.

P. tricuspidata (Boston ivy, Japanese creeper) has dark green, three-lobed leaves that turn red in fall. This species is hardy to zone 4.

P. quinquefolia (above & below)

Virginia creeper can cover the sides of buildings and help keep them cool in the summer heat. Cut the plants back to keep windows and doors accessible.

Features: summer and fall foliage; clinging habit **Height:** 30–70' **Spread:** 30–70'
Hardiness: zones 3–8

Canna Lily
Canna

C. hybrid (above & below)

Canna lilies are stunning, dramatic plants that give an exotic flair to any garden.

Growing

Canna lilies grow best in **full sun** in a **sheltered location**. The soil should be **fertile, moist** and **well drained**. Plant out in spring into warm soil. Plants can be started early indoors in containers to get a head start on the growing season. Deadhead to prolong blooming.

The rhizomes can be lifted after the foliage dies back in fall. Clean off any clinging dirt and store them in a cool, frost-free location in slightly moist peat moss. Check on them through winter, and if they start to sprout, pot them and move them to a bright window until they can be moved outdoors.

Tips

Canna lilies can be grown in a bed or border. They make dramatic specimen plants and can even be included in large planters.

Recommended

A wide range of canna lilies are available. **'Australia'** bears large, red flowers and burgundy foliage. **'Bengal Tiger'** has green-and-yellow-striped foliage and orange flowers. **'Emerald Sunset'** has ruffled, orange-red flowers and red-edged, green foliage. **Tropical Series** is a dwarf plant that is easily grown from seed. **'Tropicana'** bears orange flowers and green, pink, gold, red, burgundy and orange variegated foliage.

Features: decorative foliage; white, red, orange, pink, yellow, bicolored summer flowers **Height:** 3–6' **Spread:** 20–36"
Hardiness: zones 7–8; grown as an annual

Crocus

Crocus

C. x vernus cultivars (above & below)

Crocuses are harbingers of spring. They often appear, as if by magic, in full bloom from beneath the melting snow.

Growing

Crocuses grow well in **full sun** or **light, dappled shade**. The soil should be of **poor to average fertility, gritty** and **well drained**. The corms are planted about 4" deep in fall.

Tips

Crocuses are almost always planted in groups. Drifts of crocuses can be planted in lawns to provide interest and color while the grass still lies dormant. In beds and borders, they can be left to naturalize. Groups of plants will fill in and spread out to provide a bright welcome in spring.

Recommended

Many crocus species, hybrids and cultivars are available. The spring-flowering crocus most people are familiar with is **C. x *vernus***, commonly called Dutch crocus. Many cultivars are available with flowers in shades of purple, yellow, white, bicolored or with darker veins.

Saffron is obtained from the dried, crushed stigmas of C. sativus. *Six plants produce enough spice for one recipe. This fall-blooming plant is hardy to zone 6 and can be grown successfully in southern Illinois.*

Features: purple, yellow, white, sometimes bicolored, early-spring flowers
Height: 2–6" **Spread:** 2–4"
Hardiness: zones 3–8

Daffodil

Narcissus

Many gardeners automatically think of large, yellow, trumpet-shaped flowers when they think of daffodils, but there is a lot of variety in flower color, form and size among the daffodils.

Growing

Daffodils grow best in **full sun** or **light, dappled shade**. The soil should be **average to fertile, moist** and **well drained**. Bulbs should be planted in fall, 2–8" deep, depending on the size of the bulb. The bigger the bulb the deeper it should be planted. A rule of thumb is to measure the bulb from top to bottom and multiply that number by three to know how deeply to plant.

Tips

Daffodils are often planted where they can be left to naturalize, in the light shade beneath a tree or in a woodland garden. In mixed beds and borders, the faded leaves are hidden by the summer foliage of other plants.

Recommended

Many species, hybrids and cultivars of daffodils are available. Flowers may be 1 ½–6" across, solitary or borne in clusters. There are 12 flower form categories.

The cup in the center of a daffodil is called the corona, and the group of petals that surrounds the corona is called the perianth.

Features: white, yellow, peach, orange, pink, bicolored spring flowers **Height:** 4–24" **Spread:** 4–12" **Hardiness:** zones 3–8

Dahlia

Dahlia

The variation in size, shape and color of dahlia flowers is astonishing. You are sure to find at least one that appeals to you.

Growing

Dahlias prefer **full sun**. The soil should be **fertile, rich in organic matter, moist** and **well drained**. Tubers can be purchased and started early indoors. The tubers can also be lifted in fall and stored over the winter in slightly moist peat moss. Pot them and keep them in a bright room when they start sprouting in mid- to late winter. Deadhead to keep plants tidy and blooming.

Tips

Dahlias make attractive, colorful additions to a mixed border. The smaller varieties make good edging plants and the larger ones make good alternatives to shrubs. Varieties with unusual or interesting flowers are attractive specimen plants.

Mixed cultivars in a cutting bed (above)

Dahlias prefer cooler conditions, so the days of late summer and autumn bring out the best show of color.

Recommended

Of the many dahlia hybrids, most are grown from tubers but a few can be started from seed. Many hybrids are sold based on flower shape, such as collarette, decorative or peony-flowered. The flowers range in size from 2–12".

Features: purple, pink, white, yellow, orange, red, bicolored summer flowers; attractive foliage; bushy habit Height: 8"–5' Spread: 8–18" Hardiness: tender tuberous perennial grown as an annual

Flowering Onion
Allium

A. giganteum (above), *A. cernuum* (below)

Flowering onions, with their striking, ball-like or loose, nodding clusters of flowers, are sure to attract attention in the garden.

Growing

Flowering onions grow best in **full sun**. The soil should be **average to fertile, moist** and **well drained**. Plant bulbs in fall, 2–4" deep, depending on size of bulb.

Although the leaves have an onion scent when bruised, the flowers are often sweetly fragrant.

Tips

Flowering onions are best planted in groups in a bed or border where they can be left to naturalize. Most will self-seed when left to their own devices. The foliage, which tends to fade just as the plants come into flower, can be hidden with ground-cover or a low, bushy companion plant.

Recommended

Several flowering onion species, hybrids and cultivars have gained popularity for their decorative, pink, purple, white, yellow, blue or maroon flowers. *A. aflatunense* bears dense, globe-like clusters of lavender flowers. *A. caeruleum* (blue globe onion) has globe-like clusters of blue flowers. *A. cernuum* (nodding or wild onion) bears loose, drooping clusters of pink flowers. *A. giganteum* (giant onion) is a big plant, growing up to 6' tall, with large, globe-shaped clusters of pinky purple flowers.

Features: pink, purple, white, yellow, blue, lavender, maroon summer flowers; cylindrical or strap-shaped leaves **Height:** 1–6' **Spread:** 2–12" **Hardiness:** zones 3–8

Gladiolus

Gladiolus

Gladiolus adds an air of extravagance to the garden.

Growing

Gladiolus grows best in **full sun** but tolerates partial shade. The soil should be **fertile, humus rich, moist** and **well drained**. Flower spikes may need staking and a shelter from the wind to prevent them from blowing over.

Plant corms 4–6" deep in spring, once the soil has warmed. Corms can also be started early indoors. Plant a few corms each week for about a month to prolong the blooming period.

Tips

Planted in groups in beds and borders, gladiolus makes a bold statement. Corms can also be pulled up in fall and stored in damp peat moss in a cool, frost-free location for the winter.

Recommended

G. callianthus (Abyssinian glads) bears purple-marked, fragrant, white flowers.

G. communis (Byzantine glads) is a compact, vigorous plant that produces large clusters of magenta red flowers and lots of cormlets.

G. x *hortulanus* Grandiflorus (above)
G. 'Homecoming' (below)

G. x *hortulanus* is a huge group of hybrids. Gladiolus flowers come in almost every imaginable shade, except blue. **Grandiflorus** is the best-known group, each corm producing a single spike of large, often-ruffled flowers. **Nanus**, the hardiest group, survives in zone 3 with protection and produces several spikes of up to seven flowers. **Primulinus** produces a single spikeof up to 23 flowers.

Features: brightly colored, mid- to late-summer flowers **Height:** 18"–6' **Spread:** 6–12" **Hardiness:** zone 8; grown as an annual

Lily
Lilium

L. Asiatic Hybrids (above)
Oriental Hybrid 'Stargazer' (below)

Lily bulbs should be planted in fall before the first frost, but they can also be planted in spring if bulbs are available.

Decorative clusters of large, richly colored blooms grace these tall plants. Flowers are produced at differing times of the season depending on the hybrid, and it is possible to have lilies blooming all season if a variety of cultivars are chosen.

Growing

Lilies grow best in **full sun** but like to have their **roots shaded**. The soil should be **rich in organic matter, fertile, moist** and **well drained**.

Tips

Lilies are often grouped in beds and borders and can be naturalized in woodland gardens and near water features. These plants are narrow but tall; plant at least three plants together to create some volume.

Recommended

The many species, hybrids and cultivars available are grouped by type. Visit your local garden center to see what is available. The following are two popular groups of lilies. **Asiatic Hybrids** bear clusters of flowers in early summer or mid-summer and are available in a wide range of colors. **Oriental Hybrids** bear clusters of large, fragrant flowers in mid- and late summer. Colors are usually white, pink or red.

Also called: oriental lily **Features:** early, mid- or late-season flowers in shades of orange, yellow, peach, pink, purple, red, white **Height:** 2–5' **Spread:** 12" **Hardiness:** zones 4–8

Tulip
Tulipa

T. hybrids (above & below)

Tulips, with their beautiful, often garishly colored flowers are a welcome sight as we enjoy the warm days of spring.

Growing

Tulips grow best in **full sun**. In light or partial shade, the flowers will bend toward the light. The soil should be **fertile** and **well drained**.

Plant bulbs in fall, 4–6" deep, depending on size of bulb. Cold-treated bulbs can be planted in spring. Although tulips can repeat bloom, many hybrids perform best if planted new each year. Species and older cultivars are the best choice for naturalizing.

Tips

Tulips provide the best display when mass planted or planted in groups in flowerbeds and borders. They can also be grown in containers and can be forced to bloom early in pots indoors. Some of the species and older cultivars can be naturalized in meadow and wildflower gardens.

Recommended

There are about 100 species of tulips and thousands of hybrids and cultivars. They are generally divided into 15 groups based on bloom time and flower appearance. They come in dozens of shades, with many bicolored or multi-colored varieties. Blue is the only shade not available. Check with your local garden center in early fall for the best selection.

Features: spring flowers **Height:** 6–30"
Spread: 2–8" **Hardiness:** zones 3–8; often treated as an annual

Basil

Ocimum

The sweet, fragrant leaves of fresh basil add a delicious licorice-like flavor to salads and tomato-based dishes.

Growing

Basil grows best in a **warm, sheltered location** in **full sun**. The soil should be **fertile, moist** and **well drained**. Pinch tips regularly to encourage bushy growth. Plant out or direct sow seed after frost danger has passed in spring.

Tips

Although basil will grow best in a warm spot outdoors, it can be grown successfully in a pot by a bright window indoors to provide you with fresh leaves all year.

Recommended

O. basilicum is one of the most popular of the culinary herbs. There are dozens of varieties, including ones with large or tiny, green or purple and smooth or ruffled leaves.

O. basilicum 'Genovese' (above & below)

Basil is a good companion plant for tomatoes—both like warm, moist growing conditions, and when you pick tomatoes for a salad you'll also remember to include a few sprigs or leaves of basil.

Features: fragrant, decorative leaves
Height: 12–24" **Spread:** 12–18"
Hardiness: tender annual

Chives

Allium

The delicate, onion flavor of chives is best enjoyed fresh. Mix chives into dips or sprinkle them on salads and baked potatoes.

Growing

Chives grow best in **full sun**. The soil should be **fertile, moist** and **well drained**, but chives adapt to most soil conditions. These plants are easy to start from seed, but they do like the soil temperature to stay above 66° F before they will germinate, so seeds started directly in the garden are unlikely to sprout before early summer.

Tips

Chives are decorative enough to be included in a mixed or herbaceous border and can be left to naturalize. In an herb garden, chives should be given plenty of space to allow self-seeding.

Recommended

A. schoenoprasum forms a clump of bright green, cylindrical leaves. Clusters of pinky purple flowers are produced in early and mid-summer. Varieties with white or pink flowers are available.

A. schoenoprasum (above & below)

Chives will spread with reckless abandon as the clumps grow larger and the plants self-seed.

Chives are said to increase appetite and encourage good digestion.

Features: foliage; form; white, pink, purple flowers **Height:** 8–24" **Spread:** 12" or more **Hardiness:** zones 3–8

Coriander • Cilantro
Coriandrum

C. sativum (above & below)

The delicate, cloud-like clusters of flowers attract pollinating insects such as butterflies and bees as well as abundant predatory insects that will help to reduce pest insects your garden.

Coriander is a multi-purpose herb. The leaves, called cilantro and used in salads, salsas and soups, and the seeds, called coriander and used in pies, chutneys and marmalades, have distinct flavors and culinary uses. Look for varieties that are "late bolting." These will produce flavorful leaves for a longer period in the garden.

Growing
Coriander prefers **full sun** but tolerates partial shade. The soil should be **fertile, light** and **well drained**. These plants dislike humid conditions and do best during a dry summer.

Tips
Coriander has pungent leaves and is best planted where people will not have to brush past it. It is, however, a delight to behold when in flower. Add a plant or two here and there throughout your borders and vegetable garden, both for the visual appeal and to attract beneficial insects.

Recommended
C. sativum forms a clump of lacy basal foliage above which large, loose clusters of tiny, white flowers are produced. The seeds ripen in late summer and fall.

Features: form; foliage; white flowers; seeds
Height: 16–24"   **Spread:** 8–16"
Hardiness: tender annual

Dill
Anethum

*D*ill leaves and seeds are probably best known for their use as pickling herbs, though they have a wide variety of other culinary uses as well.

Growing

Dill grows best in **full sun** in a **sheltered** location out of strong winds. The soil should be of **poor to average fertility, moist** and **well drained**. Sow seeds every couple of weeks in spring and early summer to ensure a regular supply of leaves. Dill should not be grown near fennel because the plants will cross-pollinate and the seeds will lose their distinct flavors.

Tips

With its feathery leaves, dill is an attractive addition to a mixed bed or border. It can be included in a vegetable garden but does well in any sunny location. It also attracts predatory insects.

Recommended

A. graveolens forms a clump of feathery foliage. Clusters of yellow flowers are borne at the tops of sturdy stems.

Dill turns up frequently in historical records as both a culinary and medicinal herb. It was used by the Egyptians and Romans, and is mentioned in the Bible.

A. graveolens (above & below)

A popular Scandinavian dish called gravalax *is made by marinating a fillet of salmon with the leaves and seeds of dill.*

Features: feathery, edible foliage; yellow summer flowers; edible seeds
Height: 2–5' **Spread:** 12" or more
Hardiness: annual

Lavender
Lavandula

L. angustifolia (above & below)

The heavenly, aromatic flowers and silvery, gray-green foliage make lavender a great accent in a mixed planting or an anchor in the herb garden.

Growing

Lavenders grow best in **full sun**. The soil should be **average to fertile, alkaline** and it must be **well drained**. Established plants are heat and drought tolerant. Protect plants from winter cold and wind. In colder areas, lavenders should be covered with mulch and, if possible, a good layer of snow.

Trim plants back in late summer and spring to keep them from becoming too woody. Never cut into old growth. New buds emerging in spring will show you how far back you can cut. Leave at least one of the new buds. Avoid heavy pruning after August to give plants time to harden off before winter.

Tips

Lavenders are wonderful, aromatic edging plants and can be used to form a low hedge. To dry the flowers, cut them when they show full color but before they open completely.

Recommended

L. angustifolia (English lavender) is an aromatic, bushy subshrub that is often treated as a perennial. From mid-summer to fall, it bears spikes of small flowers. Cultivars of varying size are available. **'Munstead'** and **'Hidcote'** are the most reliably hardy cultivars for northern areas of the state.

L. x *intermedia* (lavandin) is a hybrid of English lavender and spike lavender (*L. latifolia*). The flowers are held on long spikes.

Features: mid-summer to fall purple, pink, blue, red flowers; fragrance; foliage; habit
Height: 8–36" **Spread:** 2–4'
Hardiness: zones 5–9

Mint

Mentha

The cool, refreshing flavor of mint lends itself to tea and other hot or cold beverages. Mint sauce, made from freshly chopped leaves, is often served with lamb.

Growing

Mint grows well in **full sun** or **partial shade**. The soil should be **average to fertile, humus rich** and **moist**. These plants spread vigorously by rhizomes and may need a barrier in the soil to restrict their spread.

Tips

Mint is a good groundcover for damp spots. It grows well along ditches that may only be periodically wet. It can also be used in beds and borders, but may overwhelm less vigorous plants.

The flowers attract bees, butterflies and other pollinators to the garden.

M. x *piperita* 'Chocolate' (above)
M. x *gracilis* 'Variegata' (decorative cultivar; below)

Recommended

There are many species, hybrids and cultivars of mint. Spearmint (**M. spicata**), peppermint (**M. x piperita**) and orange mint (**M. x piperita citrata**) are three of the most commonly grown culinary cultivars. There are also more decorative varieties with variegated or curly leaves, as well as those with unusual, fruit-scented leaves.

A few sprigs of fresh mint added to a pitcher of iced tea give it an extra zip.

Features: fragrant foliage; purple, pink, white summer flowers **Height:** 6–36"
Spread: 36" or more **Hardiness:** zones 4–8

Oregano • Marjoram
Origanum

O. vulgare 'Aureum' (above & below)

In Greek, oros *means 'mountain,' and* ganos *means 'joy,' so oregano translates as 'joy of the mountain.'*

Oregano and marjoram are two of the best-known and most frequently used herbs. They are popular in stuffings, soups and stews, and no pizza is complete until it has been sprinkled with fresh or dried oregano leaves.

Growing
Oregano and marjoram grow best in **full sun**. The soil should be of **poor to average fertility, neutral to alkaline** and **well drained**. The flowers attract pollinators to the garden.

Tips
These bushy perennials make a lovely addition to any border and can be trimmed to form low hedges.

Recommended
O. majorana (marjoram) is upright and shrubby, with light green, hairy leaves. It bears white or pink flowers in summer and can be grown as an annual where it is not hardy.

O. vulgare var. *hirtum* (oregano, Greek oregano) is the most flavorful culinary variety of oregano. The low, bushy plant has hairy, gray-green leaves and bears white flowers. Many other interesting varieties of *O. vulgare* are available, including those with golden, variegated or curly leaves.

Features: fragrant foliage; white or pink summer flowers; bushy habit **Height:** 12–32" **Spread:** 8–18" **Hardiness:** zones 5–8

Parsley
Petroselinum

P. crispum (above), P. crispum var. crispum (below)

Although usually used as a garnish, parsley is rich in vitamins and minerals and is reputed to freshen the breath after garlic- or onion-rich foods are eaten.

Growing

Parsley grows well in **full sun** or **partial shade**. The soil should be of **average to rich fertility, humus rich, moist** and **well drained**. Direct sow seeds because the plants resent transplanting. If you start seeds early, use peat pots so the plants can be potted or planted out without disruption.

Tips

Parsley should be started where you mean to grow it. Containers of parsley can be kept close to the house for easy picking. The bright green leaves and compact growth habit make parsley a good edging plant for beds and borders.

Features: attractive foliage **Height:** 8–24"
Spread: 12–24" **Hardiness:** zones 5–8;
grown as an annual

Recommended

P. crispum forms a clump of bright green, divided leaves. This plant is biennial but is usually grown as an annual. Cultivars may have flat or curly leaves. Flat leaves are more flavorful and curly are more decorative. Dwarf cultivars are also available.

Parsley leaves make a tasty and nutritious addition to salads. Tear freshly picked leaves and sprinkle them over your mixed greens.

Rosemary

Rosmarinus

The needle-like leaves of rosemary are used to flavor a wide variety of culinary dishes, including chicken, pork, lamb, rice, tomato and egg dishes.

Growing

Rosemary prefers **full sun** but tolerates partial shade. The soil should be of **poor to average fertility** and **well drained**.

Tips

Rosemary is often grown in a shrub border where hardy. In Illinois, it is usually grown in a container as a specimen or with other plants. Low-growing, spreading plants can be included in a rock garden or along the top of a retaining wall and can be grown in hanging baskets.

R. officinalis (above & below)

Recommended

R. officinalis is a dense, bushy, evergreen shrub with narrow, dark green leaves. The habit varies somewhat between cultivars, from strongly upright to prostrate and spreading. Flowers are usually in shades of blue, but pink-flowered cultivars are available. Cultivars are available that can survive in zone 6 in a sheltered location with winter protection. Plants rarely reach their mature size when grown in containers.

To overwinter a container-grown plant, keep it in very light or partial shade in summer, then put it in a sunny window indoors for winter and keep it well watered but not soaking wet.

Features: fragrant, evergreen foliage; bright blue, sometimes pink, summer flowers
Height: 8"–4' **Spread:** 1–4'
Hardiness: zone 8

Sage

Salvia

Sage is perhaps best known as a flavoring for stuffings, but it has a great range of uses, including in soups, stews, sausages and dumplings.

Growing

Sage prefers **full sun** but tolerates light shade. The soil should be of **average fertility** and **well drained**. These plants benefit from a light mulch of compost each year. They are drought tolerant once established.

Tips

Sage is an attractive plant for borders; it can be used to add volume to the middle, as an edging or as a feature plant near the front. Sage can also be grown in mixed planters.

Recommended

S. officinalis is a woody, mounding plant with soft gray-green leaves. Spikes of light purple flowers appear in early and mid-summer. Many cultivars with attractive foliage are available, including the silver-leaved **'Berggarten,'** the purple-leaved **'Purpurea,'** the yellow-margined **'Icterina,'** and the purple-green and cream variegated **'Tricolor,'** which has a pink flush to the new growth.

S. officinalis 'Icterina' (above)
S. officinalis 'Purpurea' (below)

Sage has been used since at least ancient Greek times as a medicinal and culinary herb and continues to be widely used for both those purposes today.

Features: fragrant decorative foliage; blue or purple summer flowers **Height:** 12–24" **Spread:** 18–36" **Hardiness:** zones 4–7

Thyme
Thymus

T. vulgaris (above), T. x citriodorus (below)

Thyme is a popular culinary herb used in soups, stews, casseroles and with roasts.

Growing

Thyme prefers **full sun**. The soil should be **neutral to alkaline** and of **poor to average fertility**. **Good drainage** is essential. It is beneficial to work leaf mold and sharp limestone gravel into the soil to improve structure and drainage.

Tips

Thyme is useful for sunny, dry locations at the front of borders, between or beside paving stones, on rock gardens and rock walls, and in containers.

Once the plants have finished flowering, shear them back by about half to encourage new growth and to prevent the plants from becoming too woody.

Recommended

T. **x** *citriodorus* (lemon-scented thyme) forms a mound of lemon-scented, dark green foliage. The flowers are pale pink. Cultivars with silver- or gold-margined leaves are available.

T. **vulgaris** (common thyme) forms a bushy mound of dark green leaves. The flowers may be purple, pink or white. Cultivars with variegated leaves are available.

These plants are bee magnets when blooming; thyme honey is pleasantly herbal and goes very well with biscuits.

Features: bushy habit; fragrant, decorative foliage; purple, pink, white flowers
Height: 8–16" **Spread:** 8–16"
Hardiness: zones 4–8

Artemisia
Artemisia

The foliage of artemisias provides wonderful contrast and texture to the perennial border.

Growing

Artemisias grow best in **full sun**. The soil should be of **average to high fertility** and **well drained**. They dislike wet, humid conditions.

Artemisias respond well to pruning in late spring. If you prune before May, frost may kill any new growth. Cut straggly-looking plants back hard to encourage new growth and to maintain a neater form. Divide every year or two when the plants thin in their centers.

Tips

Use artemisias in rock gardens and borders. Their silvery gray foliage makes them good backdrop plants to use behind brightly colored flowers or to fill in spaces between other plants. Smaller forms may be used to create knot gardens.

Recommended

A. absinthium (wormwood) is a clump-forming, woody-based plant with aromatic, hairy, silvery gray foliage. (Zones 4–8)

A. stelleriana 'Silver Brocade' (above)
A. ludoviciana 'Valerie Finnis' (below)

A. lactiflora (white mugwort) is an upright, clump-forming plant with dark green foliage and large panicles of creamy white flowers. (Zones 4–8)

A. ludoviciana (white sage, silver sage) cultivars are upright, clump-forming plants with silvery white foliage. (Zones 4–8)

A. schmidtiana (silvermound artemisia) is a low, dense, mound-forming perennial with feathery, hairy, silvery gray foliage. 'Nana' grows only half the size of the species.

A. stelleriana 'Silver Brocade' is a low, somewhat spreading cultivar with soft, pale gray leaves.

Also called: wormwood, sage **Features:** silvery gray, feathery or deeply lobed foliage
Height: 6"–6' **Spread:** 12–36"
Hardiness: zones 3–8

Bishop's Hat
Epimedium

E. x youngianum 'Niveum' (above), *E. x rubrum* (below)

Plant bishop's hat in a location where the beautiful foliage and flowers are easily seen, especially in fall.

Growing
Bishop's hat prefers **partial sun** in **rich, moist, well-drained** soil. **Protect from cold, dry winds**. Most varieties are drought tolerant. Apply thick mulch in mid- to late fall, whether snow coverage is reliable or not, to provide a protective barrier and maintain adequate moisture in the soil. Divide in fall.

Shear back the oldest foliage and flowers in late winter or early spring before the new flower buds emerge. This produces the best display of foliage and flowers.

Tips
Bishop's hat can be trained as a climbing vine. Without support, it serves as a groundcover in shady locations, in a woodland setting or on the side of a sheltered wall.

Recommended
E. x *rubrum* (red barrenwort) is a spreading, clump-forming plant with pink and yellow bicolored flowers. The foliage is tinged reddish green, which intensifies with age.

E. x *versicolor* forms mounds of finely divided foliage. Young foliage is coppery red, fading to green with age. The small flowers are a deep reddish pink with yellow petals. **'Sulphureum'** bears yellow flowers with long spurs.

E. x *youngianum* has green foliage and red-tinted stems. It bears white or pale pink flowers, sometimes with spurs. **'Niveum'** bears white flowers with colorful young foliage.

Features: red, pink, purple, white, yellow spring and summer flowers; attractive foliage **Height:** 8–12" **Spread:** 8–12" **Hardiness:** zones 4–8

Blue Fescue

Festuca

F. glauca 'Elijah Blue' (above), *F. glauca* (below)

Blue fescue was one of the first ornamental grasses to appear on the market over a decade ago. It continues to display its finest features in harsh conditions.

Growing

Blue fescue prefers **full sun** in **poor to moderately fertile, well-drained** soil. Keep the soil a little on the dry side.

Tips

The low-growing tufts of blue fescue are used as edging for beds and borders, and they look great when mass planted. They are frequently used in xeriscape settings and naturalized areas. The low-growing fescues also work well in rock and alpine gardens.

Recommended

F. glauca (*F. ovina* var. *glauca*; blue sheep's fescue) produces steely blue tufts of fine, needle-like blades of grass. Most varieties produce tan-colored flower spikes that rise above the mounds of blue foliage. Many cultivars and hybrids are available. **'Boulder Blue'** has very blue foliage with a metallic sheen. **'Elijah Blue'** has soft, powdery blue foliage. **'Skinner's Blue'** has soft, blue-gray foliage. **'Solling'** has blue-gray leaves that turn shades of reddish brown in fall. It does not bear flowers.

Fescue specimens can be divided every two or three years, or when they begin to die out in the centers. This will help to maintain the foliage color.

Features: colorful foliage; flower spikes; growth habit **Height:** 6–18" **Spread:** 10–12" **Hardiness:** zones 3–8

Blue Oat Grass
Helictotrichon

H. sempervirens (above & below)

This hardy grass is the perfect plant for those who desire a super-sized version of blue fescue for their garden.

Growing
Blue oat grass thrives in **full sun**. The soil should be **average to dry** and **well drained**. This grass is considered to be evergreen, but it will still need a trim in spring to encourage new growth and to simply tidy it up.

Tips
This large, non-spreading grass is ideal for just about any setting, from beds and borders to containers. It works well in a xeriscape design or naturalized area. It is a lovely complement to flowering perennials and shrubs because of its wonderful color, impressive size and growth habit.

Recommended
H. sempervirens is a large, coarse-textured grass that produces perfectly rounded, dome-shaped clumps of intensely blue foliage. Wiry, tan stems emerge through the foliage and are tipped with tan seedheads.

Blue oat grass is easily propagated by division in early spring. It is a cool-season perennial that is a reliable Illinois dweller.

Features: brilliant blue foliage; decorative spikes of tan seedheads **Height:** 2–4' **Spread:** 24–30" **Hardiness:** zones 3–8

Bugleweed

Ajuga

A. reptans 'Catlin's Giant' (above & below)

Often labeled as a rampant runner, bugleweed grows best where it can roam freely without competition.

Growing

Bugleweed develops the best leaf color in **partial or light shade** but tolerates full shade. The leaves may become scorched when exposed to too much sun. Any **well-drained** soil is suitable. Divide this vigorous plant any time during the growing season. Remove any new growth or seedlings that don't show the hybrid leaf coloring.

Tips

Bugleweed makes an excellent ground-cover for difficult sites, such as exposed slopes and dense shade. It also looks attractive in shrub borders, where its dense growth prevents the spread of all but the most tenacious weeds.

Recommended

A. pyramidalis 'Metallica Crispa' (upright bugleweed) is a very slow-growing plant with metallic, bronzy brown, crinkly foliage and violet blue flowers.

A. reptans (common bugleweed) is a low, quick-spreading groundcover. Its many cultivars are often chosen over the species for their colorful, often variegated foliage. **'Catlin's Giant'** has large, bronze leaves and bears short spikes of bright blue flowers. **'Chocolate Chip'** is a low, creeping plant with chocolaty bronze, teardrop-shaped leaves and spikes of blue flowers.

Bugleweed combines well with hostas and ferns; it enjoys the same shady sites and growing conditions.

Features: colorful, decorative foliage; late-spring to early-summer purple, blue, pink, white flowers **Height:** 3–12" **Spread:** 6–36" **Hardiness:** zones 3–8

Caladium

Caladium

C. x hortulanum cultivar (above)
C. x hortulanum 'Sweetheart' (below)

Shade is a cross that many of us bear, and usually not cheerfully. 'More color!' is the refrain heard over and over when discussing shade. Caladium provides the solution.

Growing

Caladium prefers to grow in **partial to full shade** in **moist, well-drained, humus-rich, slightly acidic** soil.

Start tubers indoors in a soil-less planting mix with the soil temperature at 70° F. Make sure the knobby side of the tuber is facing up and is level with or just under the soil surface. Add a little bonemeal or fishmeal to the planting hole. Once plants have leafed-out, they can handle a soil temperature of 55° F.

Dig tubers in fall after the leaves die back. Remove as much soil as possible, let them dry for a few days, and store them in slightly damp peat moss at 55–60° F. If grown in a container, simply bring the whole container inside over winter.

Tips

Caladium looks great as a specimen or when mass planted. Use it around water features and in woodland gardens, herbaceous borders and containers.

All parts of caladium may irritate the skin, and ingesting this plant will cause stomach upset.

Recommended

C. x hortulanum is a complex group of hybrids with large, often tufted, arrow-shaped, dark green foliage that is variously marked and patterned with red, white, pink, green, rose, salmon, silver or bronze.

Take care if you decide to grow N. cataria (catnip) because cats are extremely attracted to this plant. Cats do like the other species, but not as much.

Features: ornate foliage; habit **Height:** 18–24" **Spread:** 18–24" **Hardiness:** tender perennial; treat as an annual

Catmint
Nepeta

N. x *faassenii* 'Walker's Low' (above), *N.* x *faassenii* (below)

Plants in the *Nepeta* genus are members of the mint family. It is not surprising that they are fragrant, nor that they spread so well they are potentially invasive.

Growing

Catmint grows well in **full sun** or **partial shade**. The soil should be of **average fertility** and **well drained**. Plants tend to flop over in fertile soil. Pinch plants back in early June to encourage bushy, compact growth. Cut back after blooming to encourage a second flush of flowers.

Tips

The lower-growing catmints can be used to edge borders and pathways and can also be used in rock gardens. Taller selections make lovely additions to perennial beds. All catmints work well in herb gardens and with roses in a cottage garden.

Recommended

N. x **faassenii** forms a clump of upright, spreading stems. Spikes of blue or lavender flowers are produced in spring and summer and sometimes again in fall. Many cultivars and hybrids are available. **'Blue Wonder'** grows 10–14" tall and 12–18" wide, and produces dense, gray-green foliage and dark blue flowers. **'Walker's Low'** has gray-green foliage and lavender blue flowers. It grows about 10" tall.

Features: blue, purple, pink, white spring or summer flowers; fragrant foliage; habit
Height: 10–36" **Spread:** 10–36"
Hardiness: zones 3–8

Coleus

Solenostemon (Coleus)

S. *scutellarioides* cultivars (above & below)

With so many color variations in the foliage, coleus traditionally was the stalwart of the shade garden. Now, colors have been improved and new varieties actually do better in sun than shade. There is a coleus for everyone.

Growing

Coleus prefers **light or partial shade** but tolerates full shade if not too dense, and full sun if it is watered regularly. The soil should be **average to fertile, humus rich, moist** and **well drained**.

Place the seeds in a refrigerator for one or two days before planting them; the cold temperature helps break seed dormancy. They need light to germinate, so leave the seeds on the soil's surface. Seedlings are green at first, with variegation developing as the plants mature.

Tips

Coleus looks dramatic when grouped in beds, borders and mixed containers, or when planted as edging.

Pinch off flower buds once they have developed. Coleus flowers tend to stretch out and become less attractive after they bloom.

Recommended

S. scutellarioides (*Coleus blumei* var. *verschaffeltii*) forms a bushy mound of multi-colored, slightly toothed to very ruffled foliage. Dozens of cultivars are available, but many cannot be started from seed. New varieties that tolerate full sun and have larger, more colorful foliage are available.

Take cuttings from a mother plant and overwinter them indoors. The cuttings root easily in a glass of water.

Features: brightly colored foliage
Height: 6–36" or more **Spread:** usually equal to height **Hardiness:** treat as an annual

Dead Nettle
Lamium

These attractive plants hug the ground and thrive on only the barest necessities of life.

Growing
Dead nettles prefer **partial to light shade** and **humus-rich, moist, well-drained** soil of **average fertility**. They grow vigorously in fertile soil. Dead nettles can develop bare patches if the soil is allowed to dry out for extended periods. Divide and replant them in fall if bare spots become unsightly.

L. maculatum 'Lime Light' (above)
L. maculatum 'Beacon Silver' (below)

Plants remain compact if sheared back after flowering. If they remain green over the winter, shear them back in early spring.

Tips
These plants make useful groundcovers for woodland or shade gardens. They work well under shrubs in a border, where they help keep weeds down.

Recommended
L. galeobdolon (*Lamiastrum galeobdolon*; yellow archangel) has yellow flowers and can be quite invasive, though the cultivars are less so. **'Herman's Pride'** forms dense mats of coarsely toothed, green foliage, heavily streaked with silver.

L. maculatum (spotted dead nettle) is a low-growing, spreading species with green leaves marked with white or silver. It bears white, pink or mauve flowers. **'Orchid Frost'** has silvery, green-edged foliage and deep pink flowers. **'White Nancy'** has white flowers and silver leaves with green margins.

If your dead nettles become invasive and overwhelm other plants, pull some of them up, making sure to remove the fleshy roots.

Features: decorative, often-variegated foliage; white, pink, yellow, mauve spring or summer flowers **Height:** 4–24" **Spread:** indefinite **Hardiness:** zones 3–8

Dusty Miller

Senecio

S. cineraria 'Cirrus' (above), *S. cineraria* (below)

Novice gardeners may look at this plant as the 'something different' in their flowerbeds. Dusty miller is easy to grow and care for. It provides good contrast in beds of colorful flowers and can be effectively worked into containers.

Growing

Dusty miller prefers **full sun** but tolerates light shade. The soil should be of **average fertility** and **well drained**.

Tips

The soft, silvery, lacy leaves of this plant is its main feature. Dusty miller is used primarily as an edging plant but is also effective in beds, borders and containers. The silvery foliage makes a good backdrop to show off the brightly colored flowers of other plants.

Pinch off the flowers before they bloom. They aren't showy and they steal energy that would otherwise go to producing more foliage.

Recommended

S. cineraria forms a mound of fuzzy, silvery gray, lobed or finely divided foliage. Many cultivars have been developed with impressive foliage colors and shapes.

Mix dusty miller with geraniums, begonias or cockscombs to bring out the vibrant colors of those flowers.

Features: silvery foliage; neat habit; easy to grow; yellow to white flowers **Height:** 12–24" **Spread:** equal to height or slightly narrower **Hardiness:** tender perennial; treat as an annual

English Ivy
Hedera

One of the loveliest things about English ivy is the variation in green and blue tones it adds to the garden.

Growing

English ivy prefers **light or partial shade** but adapts to any light conditions, from full shade to full sun. The foliage can become damaged or dried out in winter if the plant is grown in a sunny, exposed site. The soil should be of **average to rich fertility, moist** and **well drained**. The richer the soil, the better this vine will grow.

Tips

English ivy is grown as a trailing groundcover that roots at the stem nodes, or as a climbing vine. It clings tenaciously to house walls, tree trunks, stumps and many other rough-textured surfaces. Ivy rootlets can damage walls and fences, and can be invasive in warmer climates. Choose smaller-leaved cultivars for slower growth.

Recommended

H. helix is a vigorous plant with dark, glossy, triangular, evergreen leaves that may be tinged with bronze or purple in winter, adding another season of interest to your garden. Many cultivars have been developed, including some with interesting, often-variegated foliage. Check with your local garden center to see what is available.

H. helix (above & below)

Ivy is a popular houseplant and is frequently used in wire-frame topiaries.

Features: foliage; climbing or trailing habit
Height: 6–8" as a groundcover; up to 90' when climbing **Spread:** indefinite
Hardiness: zones 5–9

Flowering Fern

Osmunda

O. regalis (above), O. cinnamomea (below)

The flowering fern's 'flowers' are actually its spore-producing sporangia.

Ferns have a certain pre-historic mystique, and they add a graceful elegance and textural accent to the garden.

Growing

Flowering ferns prefer **light shade** but tolerate full sun if the soil is consistently moist. The soil should be **fertile, humus rich, acidic** and **moist**. Flowering ferns tolerate wet soil and will spread as offsets form at the plant bases.

Tips

These large ferns form an attractive mass when planted in large colonies. They can be included in beds and borders, and make a welcome addition to a woodland garden.

Recommended

O. cinnamomea (cinnamon fern) has light green fronds that fan out in a circular fashion from a central point. Bright green, leafless, fertile fronds that mature to cinnamon brown are produced in spring and stand straight up in the center of the plant.

O. regalis (royal fern) forms a dense clump of foliage. Feathery, flower-like, fertile fronds stand out among the sterile fronds in summer and mature to a rusty brown. **'Purpurescens'** fronds are purpled-red when they emerge in spring and then mature to green. This contrasts well with the purple stems. (Zones 3–8)

Features: perennial deciduous fern; decorative, fertile fronds; habit **Height:** 30"–5' **Spread:** 24–36" **Hardiness:** zones 2–8

Fountain Grass

Pennisetum

P. setaceum 'Rubrum' (left)
P. glaucum 'Purple Majesty' (above)

Fountain grass' low maintenance and graceful form make it easy to place. It will soften any landscape, even in winter.

Growing

Fountain grass thrives in **full sun** in **well-drained** soil of **average fertility**. Plants are drought tolerant once established. They may self-seed but are not troublesome. Shear perennials back in early spring, and divide them when they start to die out in the center.

Tips

Fountain grasses can be used as individual specimen plants and in group plantings and drifts, or can be combined with flowering annuals, perennials, shrubs and other ornamental grasses. Annual selections are often planted in containers.

Recommended

P. alopecuroides 'Hameln' (dwarf perennial fountain grass) is a compact cultivar with silvery white plumes and narrow, dark green foliage that turns gold in fall. **'Little Bunny'** is the smallest of all dwarf fountain grasses. **'Moudry'** has wider, dark green leaves and very dark purple flowers.

P. glaucum **'Purple Majesty'** (purple ornamental millet) is an annual bearing blackish purple foliage and coarse, bottlebrush flowers.

P. setaceum (annual fountain grass) has narrow, green foliage and pinkish purple flowers that mature to gray. **'Rubrum'** (red annual fountain grass) has broader, deep burgundy foliage and pinkish purple flowers.

Features: arching, fountain-like habit; silvery pink, dusty rose to purplish black foliage; flowers; winter interest **Height:** 2–5' **Spread:** 24–36" **Hardiness:** zones 5–8 or annual

The name Pennisetum *refers to the plume-like flower spikes. In Latin,* penna *means feather, and* seta *means bristle.*

Golden Hakone Grass

Hakonechloa

H. macra 'Aureola' (above & below)

Golden Hakone grass is an attractive, shade-loving grass that provides interest throughout the growing season.

Growing

Golden Hakone grass prefers **light or partial shade** in **fertile, moist, well-drained** soil that is **rich in organic matter**. It tolerates full sun if the soil is kept moist. Use mulch to maintain soil moisture as these plants resent drying out. If the foliage becomes scorched, move the plant to a more shaded location. Mulch in winter to protect the plants.

Tips

The texture and color of golden Hakone grass is a good contrast to broad-leaved shade plants. It makes an attractive addition to mixed beds and borders, and can be used along the tops of retaining walls where its arching habit will show well.

Recommended

H. macra has bright green, arching, grass-like foliage that turns deep pink in fall, then changes to bronze as winter sets in. '**Albo-Striata**' has green-and-white-striped leaves. '**All Gold**' has pure gold leaves and is more upright and spiky in habit. '**Aureola**' has bright yellow foliage with narrow, green streaks; the foliage turns pink in fall. Yellow-leaved cultivars may scorch in full sun and lose their yellow color in too much shade.

Golden Hakone grass is native to Japan, where it grows on mountainsides and cliffsides, often near streams and other water sources.

Features: fall color; arching habit
Height: 12–24" **Spread:** 12–24"
Hardiness: zones 5–9

Lungwort
Pulmonaria

*L*ightening up shady nooks is always a challenge and is one reason lungworts find their way into so many gardens. Favorite selections from the Chicago Botanic Garden include 'Tim's Silver,' *P. saccharata* 'Sissinghurst White' and the smaller *P. longifolia* 'Bertram Anderson.'

Growing

Lungworts prefer **partial to full shade**. The soil should be **fertile, humus rich, moist** and **well drained**. Rot can occur in very wet soil.

Divide in early summer after flowering or in fall. Provide the newly planted divisions with lots of water to help them re-establish. Deadhead to keep the plants tidy.

Tips

Lungworts make useful and attractive groundcovers for shady borders, woodland gardens and pond and stream edges.

Recommended

P. longifolia (long-leaved lungwort) is a dense plant with long, narrow, white-spotted green leaves and clusters of blue flowers.

P. officinalis (common lungwort, spotted dog) forms a loose clump of evergreen foliage, spotted with white. The flowers open pink and mature to blue. Cultivars are available.

P. saccharata (above & below)

P. saccharata (Bethlehem sage) has large, white-spotted, evergreen leaves and purple, red or white flowers. Many cultivars are available.

P. **'Tim's Silver'** has spotted foliage that appears almost totally silver.

This plant has more than 20 common names, many of which are biblical references.

Features: decorative, mottled foliage; blue, red, pink, white spring flowers **Height:** 8–24"
Spread: 8–36" **Hardiness:** zones 3–8

Maidenhair Fern

Adiantum

A. pedatum (above & below)

These charming and delicate-looking native ferns add a graceful touch to any woodland planting. Their unique habit and texture will stand out in any garden.

Growing

Maidenhair fern grows well in **light or partial shade** but tolerates full shade. The soil should be of **average fertility, humus rich, slightly acidic** and **moist**. This plant rarely needs dividing, but it can be divided in spring to propagate more plants.

Tips

These lovely ferns will do well in any shaded spot. Include them in rock gardens, woodland gardens, shaded borders and beneath shade trees. They also make an attractive addition to a shaded planting next to a water feature or on a slope where the foliage can be seen when it sways in the breeze.

Recommended

A. pedatum is a deciduous perennial fern that forms a spreading mound of delicate, arching fronds. Light green leaflets stand out against the black stems, and the whole plant turns bright yellow in fall. Spores are produced on the undersides of the leaflets.

Also called: northern maidenhair fern
Features: summer and fall foliage; habit
Height: 12–24" **Spread:** 12–24"
Hardiness: zones 2–8

Miscanthus

Miscanthus

Miscanthus is one of the most popular and majestic of all the ornamental grasses. Its graceful foliage dances in the wind and makes an impressive sight all year long.

Growing

Miscanthus prefers **full sun**. The soil should be of **average fertility, moist** and **well drained**, though some selections tolerate wet soil. All selections are drought tolerant once established.

Tips

Give these magnificent beauties room to spread so you can fully appreciate their form. The plant's height will determine the best place for each selection in the border. They create dramatic impact in groups or as seasonal screens.

Recommended

There are many available cultivars of **M. *sinensis***, all distinguished by the white midrib on the leaf blade. Some popular selections include **'Gracillimus'** (maiden grass), with long, fine-textured leaves; **'Grosse Fontaine'** (large fountain), a tall, wide-spreading, early-flowering selection; **'Morning Light'** (variegated maiden grass), a short, delicate plant with fine, white leaf edges; **var. *purpurescens*** (flame grass), with foliage that turns bright orange in early fall; and **'Strictus'** (porcupine grass), a tall, stiff, upright selection with unusual, horizontal yellow bands.

M. sinensis var. *purpurescens* (above)
M. sinensis cultivar (below)

Also called: eulalia, Japanese silver grass
Features: upright, arching habit; colorful summer and fall foliage; pink, copper, silver late-summer and fall flowers; winter interest
Height: 4–8' **Spread:** 2–4'
Hardiness: zones 5–8, possibly zone 4

Ostrich Fern

Matteuccia

M. struthiopteris (above & below)

Ostrich ferns are also grown commercially for their edible fiddleheads. The tightly coiled, new spring fronds taste delicious lightly steamed and served with butter. Remove the bitter, reddish brown, papery coating before steaming.

These popular, classic ferns are revered for their delicious, emerging spring fronds and their stately, vase-shaped habit.

Growing

Ostrich fern prefers **partial or light shade** but tolerates full shade, and even full sun if the soil is kept moist. The soil should be **average to fertile, humus rich, neutral to acidic** and **moist**. Leaves may scorch if the soil is not moist enough. These ferns are aggressive spreaders that reproduce by spores. Unwanted plants can be pulled up and composted or given away.

Tips

Ostrich fern appreciates a moist woodland garden and is often found growing wild alongside woodland streams and creeks.

Useful in shaded borders, this plant is quick to spread, to the delight of those who enjoy the young fronds as a culinary delicacy.

Recommended

M. struthiopteris (*M. pennsylvanica*) is a hardy perennial fern that forms a circular cluster of slightly arching, feathery fronds. Stiff, brown, fertile fronds, covered in reproductive spores, stick up in the center of the cluster in late summer and persist through winter. They are popular choices for dried arrangements.

Also called: fiddlehead fern
Features: foliage; habit **Height:** 3–5'
Spread: 12–36" or more **Hardiness:** zones 1–8

Pachysandra

Pachysandra

P. terminalis (above & below)

Low-maintenance pachysandra is one of the most popular groundcovers. Its rhizomatous rootzone colonizes quickly to form a dense blanket over the ground.

Growing

Pachysandra prefers **light to full shade** but tolerates partial shade. Any soil that is **moist, acidic, humus rich** and **well drained** is good. Plants can be propagated easily from cuttings or by division.

Tips

Pachysandras are durable groundcovers under trees, in shady borders and in woodland gardens. The foliage is considered evergreen, but winter-scorched shoots may need to be removed in spring. Shear or mow old plantings in early spring to rejuvenate them.

Recommended

P. terminalis (Japanese spurge) is a perennial, evergreen groundcover that forms a low mass of foliage rosettes. It can spread almost indefinitely. **'Green Sheen'** has, as its name implies, exceptionally glossy leaves that are smaller than those of the species.

Interplant this popular groundcover with spring bulbs, hostas or ferns, or use it as an underplanting for deciduous trees and shrubs with contrasting foliage colors.

Also called: Japanese spurge
Features: inconspicuous, fragrant, white spring flowers; habit **Height:** 8" **Spread:** 12–18" or more **Hardiness:** zones 3–8

Prairie Dropseed
Sporobolus

S. heterolepis (left & above)

P rairie dropseed boasts graceful fountains of attractive, summer and fall foliage and fragrant, showy flowers. It is often visible above the snow during winter. Prairie dropseed will attract birds to your garden.

Growing
Prairie dropseed grows best in **full sun** in **rocky, well-drained** soil. It is extremely tolerant of heat and drought but appreciates occasional moisture. It also tolerates a range of soils, including heavy clay. Prairie dropseed can self-seed but is not a rampant spreader.

Sow seeds in spring or fall where they are to grow. Divide in spring or fall to propagate more plants.

Tips
Prairie dropseed is an Illinois native that is at home in meadows and native plantings. This versatile grass can be used for texture and color accents in beds, borders, containers and rock gardens. It is used effectively for erosion control and makes a great groundcover for hot, dry areas. The flowering stems make great additions to dried-flower arrangements.

Recommended
S. heterolepis is a slow-growing, long-lived, clump-forming perennial grass that has arching, very narrow, emerald green foliage that turns golden yellow with orange highlights in fall. Cloud-like clusters of pendant, fragrant, pale pink flowers are borne in late summer and are held above the mound of foliage.

Also called: rushgrass **Features:** summer and fall foliage; fragrant, airy, pink flowers; low maintenance **Height:** 18"–3 $\frac{1}{2}$' **Spread:** 24" **Hardiness:** zones 3–9

Reed Grass

Calamagrostis

This graceful grass changes its habit and flower color throughout the growing season. The slightest breeze keeps reed grass in perpetual motion.

Growing

Reed grass grows best in **full sun**. The soil should be **fertile, moist** and **well drained**, though heavy clay and dry soils are tolerated. Reed grass is susceptible to rust in cool, wet summers or in areas with poor air circulation. Rain and heavy snow may cause it to flop temporarily, but it quickly bounces back. Cut back to 2–4" in very early spring before growth begins. Divide reed grass if it begins to die out in the center.

Tips

Whether it's used as a single, stately focal point, in small groupings or in large drifts, this is a desirable, low-maintenance grass. It combines well with late-summer and fall-blooming perennials.

Recommended

C. x *acutiflora* **'Karl Foerster'** (Foerster's feather reed grass) forms a loose mound of green foliage from which airy bottlebrush flowers emerge in June. The flowering stems have a loose, arching habit when they emerge but grow stiff and upright over summer. **'Overdam'**

C. x *acutiflora* 'Overdam' (above)
C. x *acutiflora* 'Karl Foerster' (below)

is a compact, less hardy selection with white leaf edges, and **'Avalanche'** has a white center stripe.

C. arundinacea brachytricha (fall blooming reed grass) flowers much later with wider and fluffier heads and a V-shaped clump.

Features: open habit becomes upright; silvery pink flowers turn rich tan; green foliage turns bright gold in fall; winter interest
Height: 3–5' **Spread:** 24–36"
Hardiness: zones 4–9

Sedum
Sedum

S. 'Autumn Joy' (above & below)

Tips
Low-growing sedums make wonderful groundcovers and additions to rock gardens or rock walls. They edge beds and borders beautifully. Taller sedums give a lovely late-season display in a bed or border.

Recommended
S. acre (gold moss stonecrop) is a low-growing, wide-spreading plant that bears small, yellow-green flowers.

S. **'Autumn Joy'** (autumn joy sedum) is an upright hybrid whose flowers open pink or red and later fade to deep bronze.

Some 300 to 500 species of sedum are distributed throughout the Northern Hemisphere. Many are grown for their foliage, which ranges in color from steel gray-blue and green to red and burgundy.

Growing
Sedums prefer **full sun** but tolerate partial shade. The soil should be of **average fertility**, very **well drained** and **neutral to alkaline**. Divide in spring when necessary.

S. kamtschaticum is a low-growing carpet of scalloped green foliage covered with bright yellow, starry flowers.

S. spectabile (showy stonecrop) is an upright species with pink flowers. Cultivars are available.

S. spurium (two-row stonecrop) forms a low, wide mat of foliage with deep pink or white flowers. **'Bronze Carpet'** has bronze foliage and pink flowers. **'Fuldaglut'** bears red or rose pink flowers above orange-red or maroon foliage.

Also called: stonecrop **Features:** yellow, white, red, pink summer to fall flowers; decorative, fleshy foliage; easy to grow **Height:** 2–24" **Spread:** 12" to indefinite **Hardiness:** zones 3–8

Switch Grass
Panicum

A native to the prairie grasslands, switch grass naturalizes equally well in an informal border and a natural meadow.

Growing

Switch grass thrives in **full sun** or **light** or **partial shade** in **well-drained** soil of **average fertility**. It adapts to both moist and dry soils and tolerates conditions ranging from heavy clay to lighter sandy soil. Cut plants back to 2–4" from the ground in early spring. The flower stems may break under heavy, wet snow or in exposed, windy sites.

Tips

Plant switch grass singly in small gardens, in large groups in spacious borders or at the edges of ponds or pools for a dramatic effect. The seedheads attract birds, and the foliage changes color in fall.

Recommended

P. virgatum (switch grass) is suited to wild meadow gardens. **'Heavy Metal'** (blue switch grass) is an upright plant with narrow, steely blue foliage that is flushed with gold and burgundy in fall. **'Northwind'** is a compact, upright plant with blue-green foliage. **'Prairie Sky'** (blue switch grass) is an arching plant with deep blue foliage. **'Shenandoah'** (red switch grass) has red-tinged, green foliage that turns burgundy in fall.

P. virgatum 'Northwind' (above)
P. virgatum 'Heavy Metal' (below)

Switch grass' delicate, airy panicles fill gaps in the garden border and can be cut for fresh or dried arrangements.

Features: clumping habit; green, blue, burgundy foliage; airy panicles of flowers; fall color; winter interest **Height:** 3–5'
Spread: 30–36" **Hardiness:** zones 3–8

Vinca
Vinca

V. minor (above & below)

Commonly known as an evergreen groundcover plant, vinca is far more than that. Its reliability is second to none, and its ease of growth is sure to please.

Growing
Grow vinca in **partial to full shade**. It will grow in **any type of soil** but will turn yellow if the soil is too dry or the sun is too hot. Divide vinca in early spring or mid- to late fall, or whenever it is becoming overgrown. One plant can cover almost any size of area.

Tips
Vinca is an attractive groundcover in a shrub border, under trees or on a shady bank. It is shallow-rooted and able to out-compete weeds but won't interfere with deeper-rooted shrubs. It also prevents soil erosion.

Vinca can be sheared back hard in early spring. The sheared-off ends may have rooted along the stems. These rooted cuttings can be potted and given away as gifts, or can be introduced to new areas of the garden.

Recommended
V. minor forms a low, loose mat of trailing stems. Purple or blue flowers are borne in a flush in spring and sporadically throughout summer. 'Alba' bears white flowers; 'Atropurpurea' bears reddish-purple flowers; and **Bowles Series** flowers come in shades of white and blue.

Also called: lesser periwinkle, myrtle
Features: trailing foliage; purple, blue, white, reddish purple mid-spring to fall flowers
Height: 4–8" **Spread:** indefinite
Hardiness: zones 4–8

Glossary

Acid soil: soil with a pH lower than 7.0

Annual: a plant that germinates, flowers, sets seed and dies in one growing season

Alkaline soil: soil with a pH higher than 7.0

Basal leaves: leaves that form from the crown, at the base of the plant

Bract: a modified leaf at the base of a flower or flower cluster

Corm: a bulb-like, food-storing, underground stem, resembling a bulb without scales

Crown: the part of the plant at or just below soil level where the shoots join the roots

Cultivar: a cultivated plant variety with one or more distinct differences from the species, e.g., in flower color or disease resistance

Damping off: fungal disease causing seedlings to rot at soil level and topple over

Deadhead: to remove spent flowers to maintain a neat appearance and encourage a longer blooming season

Direct sow: to sow seeds directly in the garden

Dormancy: a period of plant inactivity, usually during winter or unfavorable conditions

Double flower: a flower with an unusually large number of petals

Genus: a category of biological classification between the species and family levels; the first word in a scientific name indicates the genus

Grafting: a type of propagation in which a stem or bud of one plant is joined onto the rootstock of another plant of a closely related species

Hardy: capable of surviving unfavorable conditions, such as cold weather or frost, without protection

Hip: the fruit of a rose, containing the seeds

Humus: decomposed or decomposing organic material in the soil

Hybrid: a plant resulting from natural or human-induced cross-breeding between varieties, species or genera

Inflorescence: a flower cluster

Male clone: a plant that may or may not produce pollen but that will not produce fruit, seed or seedpods

Neutral soil: soil with a pH of 7.0

Perennial: a plant that takes three or more years to complete its life cycle

pH: a measure of acidity or alkalinity; the soil pH influences availability of nutrients for plants

Rhizome: a root-like, food-storing stem that grows horizontally at or just below soil level, from which new shoots may emerge

Rootball: the root mass and surrounding soil of a plant

Seedhead: dried, inedible fruit that contains seeds; the fruiting stage of the inflorescence

Self-seeding: reproducing by means of seeds without human assistance, so that new plants constantly replace those that die

Semi-double flower: a flower with petals in two or three rings

Single flower: a flower with a single ring of typically four or five petals

Species: the fundamental unit of biological classification; the entity from which cultivars and varieties are derived

Standard: a shrub or small tree grown with an erect main stem, accomplished either through pruning and training or by grafting the plant onto a tall, straight stock

Sucker: a shoot that comes up from the root, often some distance from the plant; it can be separated to form a new plant once it develops its own roots

Tender: incapable of surviving the climatic conditions of a given region and requiring protection from frost or cold

Tuber: the thick section of a rhizome bearing nodes and buds

Variegation: foliage that has more than one color, often patched or striped or bearing leaf margins of a different color

Variety: a naturally occurring variant of a species

Index of Recommended Species Plant Names

Bold indicates main entries; *italics* represent botanical names.

Author Biographies

William Aldritch has written about gardening since 1980, mostly for the *Chicago Tribune*. He's an award-winning author of more than 20 articles and is a past president of the Garden Writers Association. A lifelong resident of the Chicago area, he founded *Chicagoland Gardening Magazine* in 1995 and remains its publisher.

Don Williamson, the coauthor of over a dozen other popular gardening guides, has a degree in horticultural technology. He has extensive experience designing and constructing beds in formal landscape settings.

Acknowledgments

Many thanks to Greg Stack of the University of Illinois Extension, the always affable Jennifer Brennan of The Chalet Nursery & Garden Center, Wilmette, and the Northern Chicagoland Rose Society.—*Bill Aldrich*

I am blessed to work with many wonderful people, including my very knowledgeable and resourceful friend Bill Aldrich, and all the great folks at Lone Pine Publishing. I also thank The Creator.—*Don Williamson*

The authors also wish to thank the following people and organizations for their valuable time and beautiful images: Allison Penko, Anne Gordon, Chicagoland Grows Inc., David Cavagnaro, Dawn Loewen, Debra Knapke, Derek Fell, Don Doucette, Duncan Kelbaugh, Erika Flatt, Jen Fafard, Joan de Grey, Kim O'Leary, Laura Peters, Leila Sidi, Marilynn McAra, Peter Thompstone, Photos.com, Robert Ritchie, Sandra Bit, Saxon Holt, Steve Nikkila, Tamara Eder, Tim Matheson, Tim Wood, Valleybrook Gardens, and all those who allowed us to photograph their gardens.